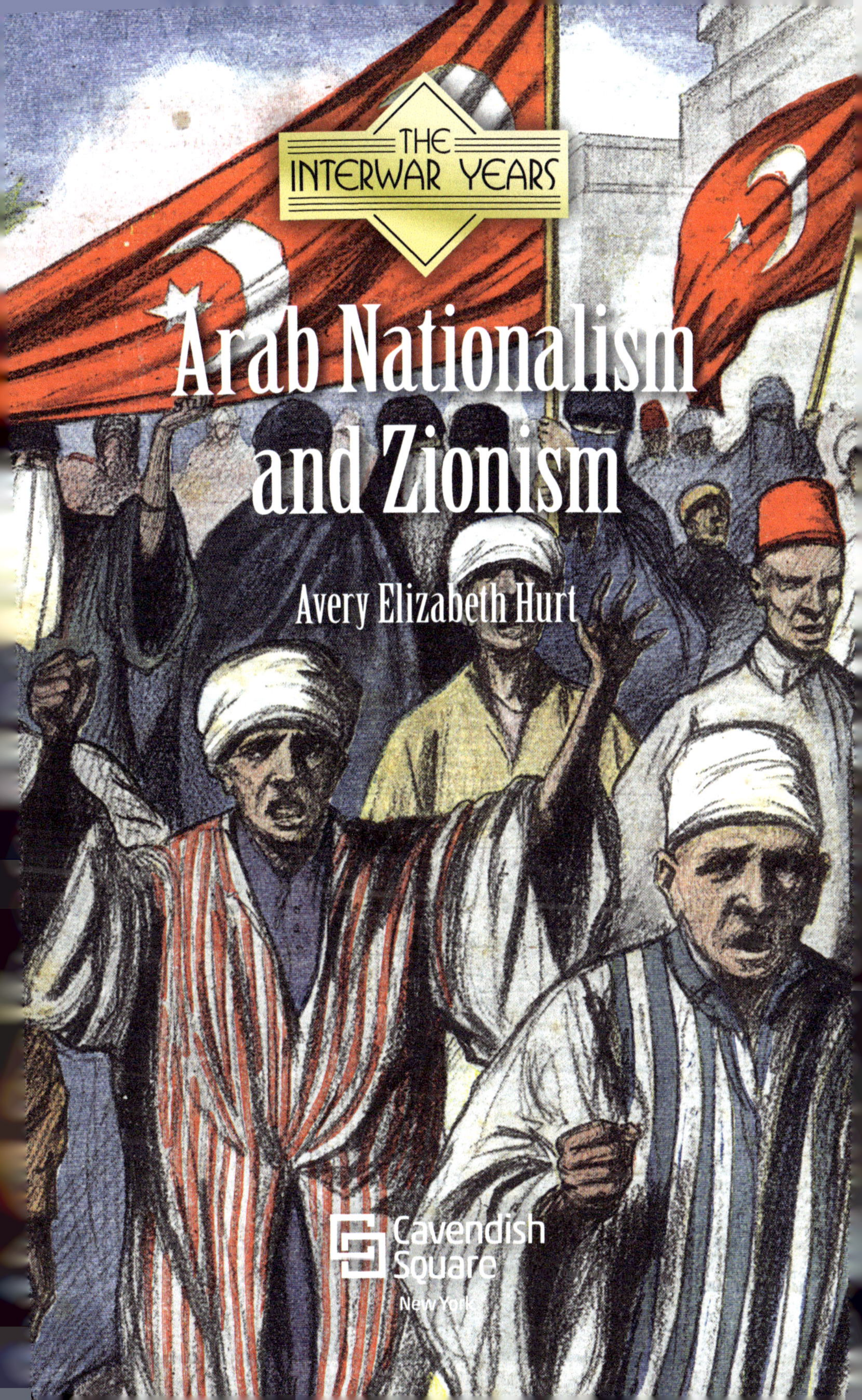

THE INTERWAR YEARS

Arab Nationalism and Zionism

Avery Elizabeth Hurt

Cavendish Square
New York

Published in 2018 by Cavendish Square Publishing, LLC
243 5th Avenue, Suite 136, New York, NY 10016

First Edition

Website: cavendishsq.com

CPSIA Compliance Information: Batch #CS17CSQ

All websites were available and accurate when this book was sent to press.

Library of Congress Cataloging-in-Publication Data

Names: Hurt, Avery, author.
Title: Arab nationalism and Zionism / Avery Elizabeth Hurt.
Description: New York : Cavendish Square Publishing, [2018] |
Series: The interwar years | Includes bibliographical references and index.
Identifiers: LCCN 2017000110 (print) | LCCN 2017001561 (ebook) |
ISBN 9781502627209 (library bound) | ISBN 9781502627155 (E-book)
Subjects: LCSH: Arab-Israeli conflict--History--Juvenile literature. | Arab nationalism--History--Juvenile literature. | Zionism--History--Juvenile literature. | Israel--History--Juvenile literature.
Classification: LCC DS119.7 .H8527 2017 (print) |
LCC DS119.7 (ebook) | DDC 320.5409569409/043--dc23
LC record available at https://lccn.loc.gov/2017000110

Editorial Director: David McNamara
Editor: Kristen Susienka
Copy Editor: Alex Tessman
Associate Art Director: Amy Greenan
Designer: Alan Sliwinski
Production Coordinator: Karol Szymczuk
Photo Research: J8 Media

The photographs in this book are used by permission and through the courtesy of: Cover, p.1 Leemage/UIG via Getty Images; p. 4 Photo12/UIG via Getty Images; p. 9 mirzavisoko/Shutterstock.com; p. 12 david156/Shutterstock.com; p. 14 George Rinhart/Corbis via Getty Images; p. 16 Kamiox/Wikimedia Commons/File:Sultan Ahmed Mosque.jpg; p. 22 Photos.com/Thinkstock; p. 24, 81 Bettmann/Getty Images; p. 27 Royal Geographical Society/Wikimedia Commons/File:MPK1-426 Sykes Picot Agreement Map signed 8; p. May 1916.jpg; p. 29 http://www.flickr.com/people/69061470@N05/Wikimedia Commons/File:Flickr - Government Press Office (GPO) -President Chaim Weizmann.jpg/CC-SA 3.0; p. 36 © Hulton-Deutsch Collection/CORBIS/Corbis via Getty Images; p. 45 Library of Congress Prints and Photographs Division Washington, D.C. 20540 USA/Wikimedia Commons/File:Mufti of Jerusalem 1931.jpg/CC-SA; p. 47 InnaFelker/Shutterstock.com; p. 50 Library of Congress; p. 52 Universal History Archive/UIG via Getty images; p. 56 Donna Ellen Coleman/Shutterstock.com; p. 60 Tom Gowanlock/Shutterstock.com; p. 66 idobi/Wikimedia Commons/File:Dome of Rock, Temple Mount, Jerusalem.jpg/CC-SA; p. 74 © Alex Gotfryd/CORBIS/Corbis via Getty Images; p. 76 Heinrich Hoffmann/Wikimedia Commons/File:Bundesarchiv Bild 146-1987-004-09A, Amin al Husseini und Adolf Hitler.jpg/CC-BY-SA 3.0; p. 85 © Hulton-Deutsch Collection/CORBIS/Corbis via Getty Images; p. 88 ullstein bild/ullstein bild via Getty Images; p. 93 Galerie Bilderwelt/Getty Images; p. 96 Sonia AlvesPolidori/Shutterstock.com; p. 102 SHERSHEL FRANK/Wikimedia Commons/File: Exodus_1947_after_British_takeover.jpg; p. 107 Hulton-Deutsch/Hulton-Deutsch Collection/Corbis via Getty Images; p. 109 Popperfoto/Getty Images; p. 113 Rainer Lesniewski/Shutterstock.com.

Printed in the United States of America

Contents

INTRODUCTION

Stirrings of Nationalism

The world we live in today has been shaped by two great nationalist movements of the late nineteenth and early twentieth centuries. Those movements are known as Arab nationalism and **Zionism**. Even now, in the twenty-first century, their impact continues to be seen on a global scale.

Nationalism is an **ideology** that unites a nation, or a group of people who would like to be a nation, by emphasizing the language, history, culture, or religion that these people share. Nationalism often reinforces these commonalities by defining the nation in terms of others who are *not* a part of it (both within and outside the nation, if that nation has a geographic location). People who do not speak the language, worship the same gods, or trace their ancestry back to the same place may not only be excluded from membership in

Opposite: *Suleiman the Magnificent was the sultan of the Ottoman Empire from 1520 to 1566.*

the nation, but by their very differences they help define the standards for that nation. Modern liberal democracies generally have very open and fluid criteria for who is and is not a part of their nations. That is why immigrants can so quickly become a part of their new homes—even without giving up their own languages or cultural traditions. However, in some nations, strict rules for who are and are not a part of the group are enforced, and that type of nationalism can sometimes become extreme.

By some definitions, a group of people does not have to occupy the same territory to be a nation. Others believe that not only a cultural identity (as would be the case with a shared language and history, for example) but a political identity is also required for a nation to exist. A political identity is created by independent control of a specific territory.

Arab Nationalism and Zionism

In the case of the Arabs of the early 1900s, the territory existed and Arabs lived there—the territory just wasn't under the independent and free control of the people who lived there. In the case of the Jewish **diaspora** during that time, the land that they considered their national home was not under Jewish control, and relatively few of the world's Jews lived there. In trying to secure a home for the people they considered a part of their nation, both nationalist movements had to contend with powerful governments whose interests often overlapped their own interests, but just as often diverged from theirs. The story of how these two nationalist movements grew and changed and shaped our history—and in some ways are still shaping the world today—is full of drama and passion and treachery.

Arabs at the End of the Ottoman Empire

The rise of Arab nationalism is often described as a response to Western **imperialism** that followed World War I, and as we shall see in coming chapters, that was a huge factor. However, there was an emerging Arab nationalist movement even before World War I began.

The Ottoman Empire—also known as the Turkish Empire—ruled what is now Turkey and most of the Middle East from the early sixteenth century until the demise of the empire at the end of World War I. For the most part, the Ottomans left the tribal clans of Arabia (including what is now Saudi Arabia) to themselves. While the Ottomans did maintain trading posts and had officials stationed in holy sites such as Medina and Mecca in Arabia, it did not interfere very much with the political and social arrangements of its subjects who lived in the interior of Arabia. The imperial government exercised somewhat more direct control over the Arab communities of Syria, Palestine, what is now Iraq, and Egypt. The people of these areas accepted the relationship, and many had roles of authority in the Ottoman administration. However, things began to change in the early twentieth century.

Near the beginning of World War I, the Ottoman Empire was beginning to weaken. A group of well-educated military officers, known as the Young Turks, had seized power in 1908 and attempted to institute reforms, such as emancipating and educating women, increasing the number of **secular** (as opposed to Islamic) courts, and ending discrimination against non-Muslims (even though the Ottoman Empire was for the most part very tolerant of non-Muslims). Little came of this movement, but it did help to further weaken the ruling structure of the empire, adding to the problems of the already-declining empire.

Other events in 1908 incited some resistance in the broader Arab population. The Ottoman government began building a railway, called the Hejaz Railway, that would link Syria's capital, Damascus, and Medina, and more importantly, provide an easy route between the capital of the Ottoman Empire, Constantinople (what is now Istanbul), and some of the holiest sites in Arabia, including Mecca and Hejaz. The Turkish rulers emphasized that the railway would ease travel for Muslims making their annual pilgrimage to Mecca, Islam's holiest site. This was indeed a benefit, but the locals quickly realized that a railroad that could take thousands of pilgrims to Mecca could also bring Ottoman soldiers, tax collectors, and other imperial officers to the interior. The days of more or less hands-off ruling seemed to be coming to an end. The clan who ruled in Hejaz, the Hashemites—leaders who could trace their ancestry back to the Prophet Muhammad—were especially disturbed by this development.

A few years later, in 1911, the al-Fatat, or the Young Arab Society, was formed. This was a nationalist movement that hoped to gain independence for Arab territories that were under Ottoman rule. This group was formed in part as a response to the Turkish nationalism of the Young Turks movement. Whereas the Young Turks were pressing for Turkish nationalism, al-Fatat wanted to protect the rights of Arabs. In 1913, a group of Arab students, academics, and journalists formed the Arab National Congress (also sometimes called the First Arab Congress or the Syrian-Arab Congress). Some historians have suggested that these revolutionaries were less concerned about the Ottoman leadership than with the intentions of Britain and France

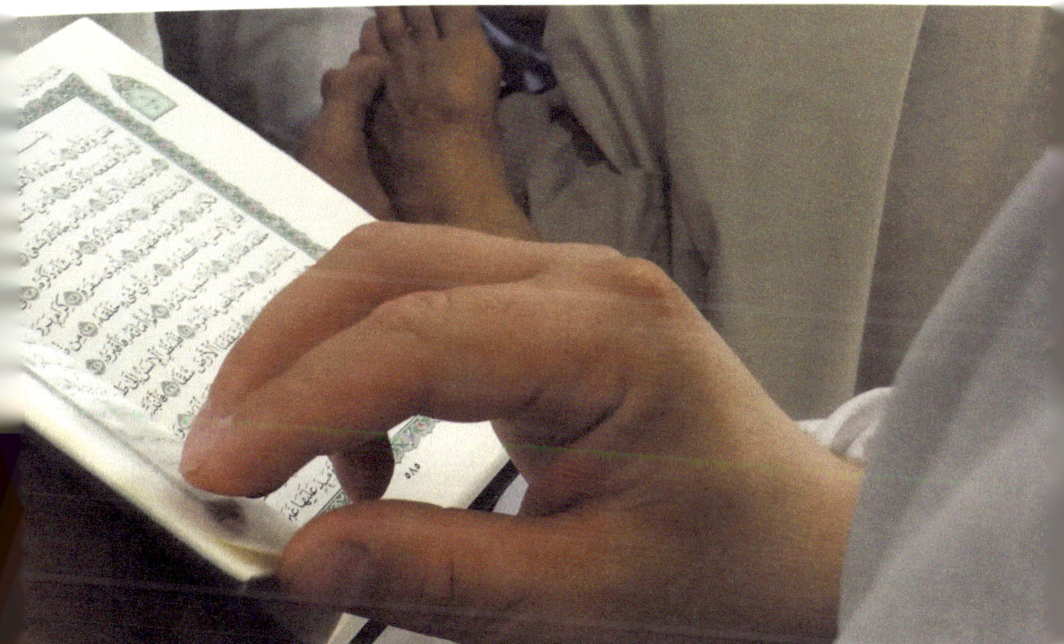

The Quran, the sacred book of Islam, was originally written in Arabic. Many Muslims today still study it in that language.

in the **Levant**. This movement spread throughout the region to some degree, but was centered in Damascus. In any case, al-Fatat had little effect other than to lay some groundwork and plant the ideological seeds for a later, more robust Arab nationalist movement.

Pride in the Arab language was a key part of the movement as well. Many Arabs felt that all people who spoke the Arabic language were culturally and spiritually connected. Muslims believe that God revealed the Quran in Arabic to an Arab (the Prophet Muhammad), giving the language a special significance to Muslims. All devout Muslims, whether or not Arabic is their native language, study and memorize the Quran in Arabic. However, as a part of the Turkish nationalist movement, many Turkish-speaking Muslims began to identify as Turks, and the Ottoman authorities, hoping to become more like a European nation state than an Islamic **caliphate**, began to enforce the use of Turkish at the expense of other languages, including Arabic. This only intensified the difficulties between Arabs and the empire.

Indeed, religion was important—but not just because of the language. As the nationalist movement began to organize, Arab leaders made the argument that the greatness of the empire was due to the Arab people's deep understanding of Islam. Though the Ottoman Empire was Islamic, throughout most of its history it had been rather accepting of other faiths and cultures, and in the years before World War I, it tolerated the development of Jewish settlements in Palestine. As it began to look more and more like the Jews were planning to organize a state, the Arab population became nervous, adding to the problems they had with the Turkish government. Other, more prosaic factors stimulated the growing nationalist impulse among the Arabs. For example, increased competition for bureaucratic appointments in the empire led to a demand for more autonomy in the Arabic-speaking provinces.

Nonetheless, though many of the tribes in the interior of Arabia had disagreements with how local problems were addressed by the Ottoman officials, most did not yet have a strong desire for Arab power. Though it was beginning to awaken, this was not yet full-fledged Arab nationalism. It's clear that stirrings of Arab nationalism had begun before the end of World War I as a resistance to Ottoman rule, but at this point, these were still minor movements. Few Arabs distinguished themselves from Turks at this time, but as the Ottoman Empire continued to decline, confidence in their leadership diminished as well, and more Arabs began to yearn to restore the great Arab civilization of the past.

This was the initial Arab Awakening within the Ottoman Empire. It did not get very far, but it did seed among the Arab subjects a lot of doubt about the legitimacy and effectiveness of the Ottoman Empire. It also alerted Western Europe to the beginnings of an Arab nationalist movement, which was skillfully, if insincerely, manipulated by the European powers during World War I.

In any event, most of these nationalist movements, as well as attempts at reform by the Young Turks, broke down and others emerged as the empire became more and more embroiled in wars, including World War I, which the Ottoman Empire entered in 1914 on the side of Germany and the **Central Powers**.

Birth of Zionism

Like Arab nationalism, Zionism also got its start well before World War I. Jewish people trace their ancestry and the founding of their religion back to Palestine. According to Jewish tradition, God gave to Abraham, the founder of Judaism, the area that is now Israel, and promised that the

An Orthodox Jewish man blows the shofar, a ceremonial ram's horn trumpet blown on special holidays.

land would belong to Abraham's descendants. Jews have lived on this land for over three thousand years; however, they have rarely been in political control of the region and were not the majority of the population there during most of history.

Besides the historical connection with the founder of Judaism, much of Jewish law and ritual is tied to the land. During the Roman occupation of the area in 70 CE, the Jewish temple in Jerusalem was destroyed and much of the Jewish population was driven from Palestine. Though many communities of Jews have continued to live there over the millennia, most Jews were forced into exile around the world, something called the diaspora. Jews were not again in political control of the area until 1948. Many Jews, even today, feel that they are in exile as long as they are living anywhere other than their homeland. Jews were very often persecuted in the lands where they settled after they left Palestine.

In the sixteenth and seventeenth centuries, several Jewish leaders emerged who urged Jews to return to Palestine. However, by the eighteenth century, there was a movement to get Jews to **assimilate** into Western secular cultures. Despite these attempts, Jews were increasingly oppressed and abused. In the late nineteenth century, a Zionist movement called the "Lovers of Zion" formed in response to **pogroms** by the czar of Russia. This group helped many Jewish farmers and tradesmen settle in Palestine.

About this time, Theodor Herzl, an Austrian journalist, began to write about and promote the idea of Zionism in Europe. While Herzl's first choice for Jews would have been assimilation, if **anti-Semitism** prevented Jews from assimilating with the cultures around them, then he felt Jews must not remain scattered around the globe, but should gather together in one territory to establish their own culture and nation. In 1897, Herzl convened the First Zionist Congress in Basel, Switzerland. The stated aim was to "create for the Jewish people a home in EretzIsrael [the land of Israel] secured by law." Though the first meeting was held in Basel (it had been originally set for Munich, but local Jews objected), the headquarters of the organization was in Vienna, Austria. After Herzl died in 1904, the headquarters moved

Early Zionists worked hard to turn the Palestine desert into productive settlements.

to Germany. It was still at that time a small movement, and was mostly made up of Russian Jews. Further pogroms in Russia created another wave of Jewish settlement in Palestine. By 1914 and the beginning of World War I, there were about ninety thousand Jews living in Palestine. Many of these Jewish settlements were funded by a Jewish French philanthropist.

Despite the growing Zionist movement, the Ottoman government, which ruled Palestine, would not agree to grant autonomy to the Jewish settlers, and the Arabs who lived in Palestine were very much opposed to Jewish settlement in their lands. In 1903, the British government offered the Zionists a large tract of uninhabited land in Uganda, but the settlers were unwilling to leave Palestine.

As a result of World War I, the British and French governments became far more involved in the nationalist movements of both the Jews and the Arabs. The politics and decisions these European powers made would have an impact on the future of both the Jewish and the Arab communities—and the rest of the world—that is still felt today.

1

Promises Made and Broken

In many ways World War I was all about imperialism. Many of the nations of Europe were trying to expand and protect their empires. The competition among these nations for territory and support from other nations often led to an astonishing amount of secret alliances, deception, and betrayal.

Setting a Stage

In 1914, at the beginning of World War I, the Ottoman Empire was the greatest independent Islamic state in the world. It lasted more than six hundred years, and at its height it covered most of southeastern Europe, almost as far north as Vienna, including what is now Hungary, Greece, the Balkans, and parts of Ukraine. In the Middle East, it held territory in

Opposite: The Sultan Ahmed Mosque in Istanbul, Turkey, was completed in 1617 during the Ottoman Empire and still is used for worship today.

what is now Iraq, Syria, Israel, Egypt, North Africa as far west as Algeria, and much of the Arab Peninsula (also called Arabia, which now includes Saudi Arabia, Yemen, Oman, Kuwait, Bahrain, Qatar, and United Arab Emirates). By the early twentieth century, however, the empire had lost much of its territory in Africa and the Balkans, and was suffering from dissent within the government.

Prior to World War I, the Ottoman Empire had been neutral toward the various factions in Europe, but when Russia mobilized forces against Germany in July 1914, the Ottoman minister of war, Enver Paşa, responded by mobilizing the Ottoman Army. On August 2, he signed a secret treaty with Germany agreeing that each country would come to the other's defense should that be necessary. The Ottoman chief minister, Said Halim Paşa, however, still wanted to remain neutral. Many government officials—particularly in the military—had close ties with Germany and with the German military, as many Ottoman officers had trained in Germany. Enver Paşa and other military leaders provoked Britain and France into declaring war on the Ottoman Empire. In response, on November 5, the **sultan** of the Ottoman Empire declared a **jihad**, or holy war, on France and Britain and officially allied his government with Germany and the Central Powers.

The pro-war elements in the Ottoman government saw the war as an opportunity to expand the empire's reach and regain territories it had recently lost in Libya and the Balkans. Ottoman leaders were also impressed with Germany's industrial and military power and hoped that an alliance with Germany would be profitable. Though the Ottoman Army was not particularly strong, in combination with Germany it posed a serious threat to the British Empire.

Britain and France Fan the Flames

Once the Ottoman Empire was in the war, Britain and France sought to further destabilize the empire by stoking nationalist sentiment among its Arabian colonies. They promised various nationalist groups that they would give them independence, and even offer to recognize an independent Arab nation at the end of the war if the Allies were victorious.

Sharif Hussein was a member of the Hashemite family, which traced its ancestry back to the Prophet Muhammad. Before the war, Sharif had quietly approached the British to see if they might be willing to support him if he should launch a revolt against the Ottoman Empire. He wanted to create a united Arab state that would include the area from Yemen to Syria, and to rule it under the principles of Islam, with himself as leader, or caliph. The British had been unwilling to commit to supporting this plan. However, after the Ottomans entered the war, the British realized that Sharif might be useful. They sent British military envoy T. E. Lawrence, now known as Lawrence of Arabia, to meet with Sharif and secure his support.

Sharif agreed to rally Arabs against the empire (and for the British). In exchange, the British offered to increase

Sharif's territory after the war and agreed to recognize Sharif as caliph if his revolt was successful. No treaty was ever signed between Britain and Sharif, but documents show that the British did promise him territory and recognition, though it is not clear whether the British ever had any intention of honoring these promises.

In any case, on June 5, 1916, forces commanded by Sharif's sons, Faisal and Ali, launched a revolt against the Ottomans. They fought on several fronts and were helpful to the British. The revolt also served to intensify nationalist feelings among the Arab population, and show them that imperial rule could be overthrown. However, the rebels who joined Sharif and his sons in the revolt had many different aims, not all of them aligning with the aims of Sharif. Some wanted a military dictatorship, and others were anarchists. There were no overarching goals for the movement, other than a desire for independence from their Turkish rulers.

Betrayal

While Sharif and his band of revolutionaries were attacking Ottoman forces, railroads, and **garrisons**, Britain and France were in the map room dividing the Arab Peninsula among themselves. The Ottoman Empire had been in decline for some time, and European governments had long considered what to do when it finally collapsed. By this time it was becoming increasingly clear that the empire would not survive World War I. In 1916, Britain and France, with the input and blessing of Russia, signed a secret agreement, called the

Sykes-Picot Agreement after the primary negotiators, Sir Mark Sykes of England and François Georges-Picot of France, that carefully spelled out what territories each nation would get after the war—areas called "spheres of influence." Britain was granted what is now Jordan, most of what is now Iraq and Kuwait, and a portion of Palestine (including what is now Israel). France got what is now Syria, Lebanon, northern Iraq, Mosul, and part of Turkey. Russia got parts of eastern Turkey. The parts of Palestine not given to the British—northern Israel and the West Bank—were to be subject to international administration, which would be determined in consultation with Russia. Much of this territory that was being parceled out among the Allies had been promised to Sharif as part of the new independent Arab nation.

This was almost a century before WikiLeaks; however, even in those days it could be difficult for governments to keep their secret machinations from the public. In 1917, a revolution overthrew the Russian government. An interim government was set up, but it, too, was overthrown in November of that year, and the **Bolsheviks**, many of whose leaders were Jewish, came to power. When the Bolsheviks took over the government, they discovered the secret Sykes-Picot Agreement among the official documents. On November 23, they published the document in Russian newspapers. A few days later, the *Manchester Guardian*, an English newspaper, picked up the story and published it as well. The cat was out of the bag. The document clearly and blatantly contradicted the agreement the British had made with the Arab leaders.

While serving as British foreign secretary, Arthur James Balfour wrote the Balfour Declaration.

Also in 1917—in fact, the very same month the Sykes-Picot Agreement was made public—the British foreign secretary, Arthur James Balfour, sent a letter to Lord Rothschild, a leader of the Jewish community in London, declaring:

"*His Majesty's Government view with favour the establishment in Palestine of a national home for the Jewish people, and will use their best endeavours to facilitate the achievement of this object, it being clearly understood that nothing shall be done which may prejudice the civil and religious rights of existing non-Jewish communities in Palestine, or the rights and political status enjoyed by Jews in any other country.*

I should be grateful if you would bring this declaration to the knowledge of the Zionist Federation."

This letter, which has come to be known as the Balfour Declaration, makes no mention of a Jewish "state," and clearly says that nothing shall be done to interfere with the rights of the non-Jewish communities in Palestine. Nonetheless, it was the first time a national power had so strongly come out in favor of a home for Jews in Palestine. The declaration raised the hopes of Zionists and became a powerful document in the movement to create a Jewish state in Palestine.

The Map Is Not the Territory

The Paris Peace Conference that settled the details of the end of World War I upheld the arrangements made by the Allies in the Sykes-Picot Agreement, despite efforts on the

LAWRENCE OF ARABIA

While on an archaeological dig in Syria, Thomas Edward Lawrence fell in love with Arab culture. Because of his extensive knowledge of the Arabic language, the young archaeologist was sent by the British military to negotiate for the help of the Arabs against the Ottoman Army during World War I, and it was he who conveyed to the Arabs the promises of the British government. Lawrence stayed and joined the fight, riding hundreds of miles across the desert, destroying railways and bridges and leading the Arabs in guerrilla attacks on the Turks.

T. E. Lawrence (left) with Lowell Thomas (right), the American journalist who made "Lawrence of Arabia" famous.

When Lawrence learned that the British weren't planning to honor their promises to the Arabs, he went to London to make the case for Arab independence. He wrote letters and newspaper articles trying to gain support for Arab independence. Dressed in Arab robes, he lobbied for Arab independence at the Paris Peace Conference at the end of the war, but was unsuccessful. In 1918, George V of England summoned Lawrence to Buckingham Palace. Lawrence hoped that the king wanted to discuss a plan for Arab independence. Instead, the king offered him a knighthood. Lawrence refused.

Lawrence was torn between loyalty to his country and loyalty to those to whom he had made promises on behalf of his government. His story is still popular today, retold in books and movies. This dashing and tragic figure is a reminder of the mistakes sometimes made by world powers and the consequences of those mistakes.

part of Sharif's son, Faisal, to persuade the allies to uphold their original agreement with Sharif.

In the spring of 1920, another conference was held, this one in San Remo, Italy, to iron out the details of the partitioning and administration of the territories of the Middle East. Representatives from Britain, France, Italy, and Japan attended, and they attempted to make some compromises. Britain and France agreed to a sort of provisional independence for the areas they had been allotted, but they retained what were called "mandates" in the region. This meant that while the territory in question was technically independent, the nation given the mandate was responsible for the "well-being and advancement of the population." Essentially, if not technically, this placed the area under the colonial rule of the nation with the mandate. How much control the area had of its own affairs was up to the country that had the mandate.

The Arab nationalists remained furious with Britain and France for reneging on their promises for land and recognition as an independent state, and this only served to reawaken the nationalist movement, which relocated to Iraq after being ousted from Syria by the French.

However, that was not the only problem created by the partition of the region. The victors had arbitrarily divided the region with little if any regard for the political communities that existed there. It is remarkable today to look at the map and notice how straight the lines are—drawn in pen across the map—that mark out the borders, as if the diplomats

The Sykes-Picot Agreement drew lines through the map of the Middle East without considering the communities that lived there.

were cutting up a cake to share between themselves, rather than defining political regions where people actually live. Syria, Lebanon, Iraq, Jordan, Palestine—these names reflect geography or classical history far more than any realistic understanding of the identities, political culture, and alliances of the people who lived there. Britain and France were concerned only with negotiating with each other for strategic influence and for access to oil. Moreover, the damage done by this lack of sensitivity is still being felt today.

On the other hand, the idea of an Arab nation was somewhat arbitrary, too. At this time, most of the people the nationalists wanted as citizens in their Arab nation did not think of themselves as Arabs as much as a part of a particular sect, religion, clan, tribe, family, or genealogy. There were Muslims and Christians, Sunnis and Shiites, **Maronites** and **Druzes**, but few people felt a very strong identity as Arabs. All these various groups did have one thing in common, though. They did not like being ruled by the British and the French. Even so, the Arab nationalist groups had trouble getting and keeping the loyalty of the people they hoped to govern. In a sense, both the colonial governments and the Arab nationalist movement were trying to impose national identity and national borders on a diverse group of people who saw themselves, their loyalties, and their boundaries in a much different way.

Growth of Zionism

Zionism also experienced a resurgence as the Ottoman Empire continued to decline and World War I began. Zionists hoped that one of the new powers in the region would support increased immigration in Palestine, and maybe eventually a Jewish state there, although Zionists made up only 12 percent of Palestine's population in 1914. On the other hand, as mentioned, the Arabs living there did not have

Chaim Weizmann was an early leader of the Zionist movement and later became the first president of Israel.

a strong sense of nationalism, and those who did espouse some kind of Arab nationalism did not agree on what form it should take.

Chaim Weizmann emerged as the leader of the Zionist movement during this period. He was a Russian-born scientist who was educated in Germany and Switzerland. He moved to London in 1905 and became a British citizen in 1910. Weizmann used his expertise in biochemistry to develop a means of producing synthetic acetone from corn. This was particularly useful to Britain in World War I because acetone was a key ingredient in certain ammunitions. Weizmann developed close ties with British leaders and used that position to influence British policy regarding Jewish settlements in Palestine. Unlike Sharif (and probably T. E. Lawrence as well), Weizmann understood that the future of the Middle East was going to be determined by the alliances, power struggles, and strategic interests of the European powers rather than the needs and desires of the people who lived in the area. The specifics of the British position were complex and, as we have seen, often contradictory.

In negotiations with Sharif and his sons, British representatives had not been completely clear about which lands would be included in the Arab kingdom promised to the nationalists in turn for their support, but it was clear that they promised land and recognition to the Arabs and that some of that land included "the Fertile Crescent in Palestine." Of course, simultaneously, the British were also negotiating with France over which country would control the very same lands. Furthermore, the Balfour Declaration made similar promises to the Zionists. Essentially, the British had made three different pledges or agreements about what would become of the Middle East when the war was over. It was obvious to Weizmann that they would not be able to keep all of their promises, but he was able to influence—at least to a degree—which policies were enacted and which remained on paper. In addition, British leaders had their own motivations for moving toward support for Zionism.

The previous British administration had not looked favorably on the Zionist cause, believing that a Jewish presence in Palestine would not be helpful for their aims in the region. Palestine had grown in importance since the war began, in part because it was close to the Suez Canal, which was of huge strategic importance to Britain. In addition to being necessary for a sea route for Persian Gulf oil, the Suez was the route for crucial troops and supplies from Australia and New Zealand, supporters of the Allies.

As the war wore on, British leaders became more and more determined that Palestine would come under British influence one way or another. By supporting the Zionist movement, the British could potentially create a strong ally that would help them protect their interests in the region. The British also hoped that by supporting the Zionists they could persuade American Jews to pressure the United States to enter the war, which was not going well for the Allies. They also hoped that the many Jews who were involved in the Bolshevik Revolution in Russia would use their influence to keep Russia in the war as well. Britain was also concerned that if they did not support the idea of some kind of Jewish community in Palestine, the Germans would.

Weizmann was aware of all these concerns and motivations, and was a talented diplomat, allowing him to play a key role in the eventual issuing of the Balfour Declaration. He worked closely with both the British Foreign Office and the British media to generate support for the Zionist cause. Meanwhile, another Zionist leader, Nahum Sokolow, was meeting with representatives of the French government and the Vatican to secure statements of support from these two powers.

Though the Balfour Declaration was short on specifics and made some conflicting promises, such as supporting a Jewish settlement while promising not to interfere with the rights of the Arabs living there, it was nonetheless a huge step for the Zionist movement. It was the first time a major world power had recognized the movement, and as such, not only gave Zionism some added legitimacy but brought it to the attention of the world. Suddenly, the idea of a Jewish homeland in Palestine seemed less like a dream and more like a political proposition.

In December 1917, just five weeks after the Balfour Declaration, Jerusalem fell to the British Army, a major setback to the Ottomans. In less than a year, all of Palestine had come under British control. Now that Britain had control of the region, it was faced with the task of hanging on to the region while keeping down a resurgence of Turkish influence, and making sure to safeguard their interests in the Suez. A homeland for the Jews became much less strategically important.

Like Faisal and Lawrence, Weizmann attended the Paris Peace Conference, and there he made his case for a Jewish state in Palestine. Weizmann and Faisal signed a separate agreement to cooperate with each other in the region, but Faisal made his cooperation contingent on Britain and France keeping their pledges. Since they did not do this, the agreement between Faisal and Weizmann was not considered

IF YOU WILL IT

Theodor Herzl is considered the founder of modern Zionism. He was born in Budapest, but moved to Vienna, Austria, when he was a teenager. After studying law in Vienna, he became a writer, journalist, and playwright. He was well educated and steeped in the secular culture of the Haskalah, an intellectual movement based on reason and rationality that encouraged Jews to study languages, science, and the arts. Followers of this movement adopted European dress and tried to assimilate into the culture of the country they lived in.

While Herzl was working as a journalist in Paris, a Jewish officer in the French army was accused of treason—as it turned out, the man was innocent. But in the wake of the accusation, many people turned on Jews. After hearing mobs in the streets shouting, "Death to the Jews," Herzl became convinced that the only way Jews would be assured of safety would be if they immigrated to a land of their own where they could found a nation and live in peace. He proposed a practical plan, including a system of funding, for making this dream come true.

Herzl worked for the rest of his life for the Zionist cause. In Vienna in 1904, he died of pneumonia that some thought may have been brought on by overwork on the Zionist cause. He did not live to see the establishment of the nation of Israel, but in 1949, his remains were reburied there. His phrase, *Wenn ihr wollt, ist es kein Märchen*, often translated as "If you will it, it is no dream," became the motto of the Zionist movement.

binding by Arab leaders. Later, at the San Remo Conference, when the specifics about the Middle East would be worked out, the British Mandate specified a "Jewish national home" in Palestine. This was a big win for Zionism, but there was still a lot of work to do before a "Jewish national home" could be translated into a nation state for the Jewish people.

A Hard Life in Palestine

Prior to World War I, the Ottoman Empire had been opposed to Zionism; however, they did allow Jewish settlements in Palestine. They had made a great deal of what were then called "capitulations" to Jewish settlers. These basically allowed Jews to immigrate to the empire but still be exempt from paying taxes and from serving in the Ottoman Army. When the war began, though, the Ottomans changed the rules. Now Jews who had come from countries that were fighting against the empire had to accept status as subjects of the Ottoman Empire, which required them to pay taxes and serve in the military, or risk being deported as citizens of enemy nations.

Many Jews were rounded up on the streets for deportation or induction into the Ottoman Army. David Ben-Gurion, who was later to become Israel's first prime minister, was one of the Jews deported under the new policy. In addition, the Ottomans repressed the use of Hebrew and **Yiddish**, the languages spoken by the Jews. The Jewish population in Palestine dropped by as much as a third during this period.

Weizmann made his first visit to Palestine in 1907. He was impressed by the hard work of the settlers there, many of them living in communes and dealing with difficult conditions. There was a great deal of poverty, and the settlers were dependent on the charity of the world Jewish community. Weizmann saw the need to improve the community—for example, by developing industry and building a university, as well as the need to cultivate political solutions with the leaders in Europe. This two-pronged approach came to be known as Synthetic Zionism.

Between 1918 and 1921, Jewish settlement and organization in Palestine was managed by the Zionist Commission. In addition to very practical advancements, such as the purchase and development of land and the development of industry, this was a period in which the Jewish community nurtured concepts such as civil rights, a sense of national identity, democracy, and political liberty—all important steps for the eventual establishment of a nation state. In 1918, Weizmann was named head of the Jewish organization and given the responsibility of implementing the Balfour Declaration. He returned to Palestine in this capacity and was disturbed to see how much the Jewish settlement had suffered during the war, though he was pleased to see so much rebuilding going on.

While the Zionist movement in Europe was doing the political and diplomatic work necessary to make the state of Israel a political possibility, the settlers were doing the work on the ground necessary to make that nation a reality.

2

Nationalism After the War

After World War I was over, and once the peace treaties had been signed and the details settled, Arab nationalists discovered that an agreement they thought guaranteed support for their aims actually undermined them in several ways. However, that wasn't the only problem they faced. It proved far more difficult in reality to keep the assorted Arab groups moving in the same direction. Most Arabs were not committed to any kind of nationalism, and those who were had many different ideas of what that should be. Some thought that the Arabic language was the most important factor; others thought that the Islamic religion was what tied all Arabs together; and others hoped for a more liberal, modern type of nation, with secularism as a defining characteristic. The Arab nationalist movement at this time encompassed several movements.

Opposite: *Many Arab soldiers fought with the British during World War I in the hopes of being granted land and nation status when the Allies prevailed.*

Creating Unity

While the people who lived throughout the region had differing ideas of what an Arab nation might be, the movement's leaders' ideas of how an Arab nation might be defined were evolving. Those changes may have been driven at least in part by the difficulty of uniting everyone.

In general, the leaders of the movement began shifting away from the idea of the nation as a voluntary contract between the government and the governed, and moving toward a notion of something more in line with the prevailing German idea of nation: that a nation was naturally formed by the language, history, and traditions of the people that made up that nation. While this was not that different from their idea of some kind of **pan-Arab** unity, it did have one subtle difference. The previous idea of Arab nationalism had emphasized a unity desired by the people themselves, but this new idea was that unity existed whether the people realized it or not, and might have to be imposed on those people if they did not understand the importance of it. The unity of the nation became more important than the freedom of the people who made up that nation.

While democracy and self-rule had been an integral part of the Arab nationalist movement, those aspects were easy enough to set aside if that was the only way to bring the nation into existence. Sati al-Husri, one of the most influential thinkers of the Arab nationalist movement, wrote:

> *Every person who speaks in Arabic is an Arab. Everyone who is affiliated with these people is an Arab. If he does not know this or if he does not cherish his Arabism, then we must study the reasons for his position. It may be the result of ignorance—then we must teach him the truth. It may be because he is unaware or deceived—then we must awaken him and reassure him. It may be a result of selfishness—then we must work to limit his selfishness.*

By this time, the nationalists were struggling not only with the imperialists who wanted control of their lands but also with many of the people who lived there. It was not the first time and would not be the last that a revolutionary movement found itself needing to "re-educate" the people it hoped to liberate.

France Cracks Down in Syria

In 1918, Sharif's son Faisal established the Kingdom of Syria as an independent Arab constitutional government and claimed authority over all of Syria. The Syrian Congress also claimed Palestine, Lebanon, and Mesopotamia (what is now Iraq) for King Faisal. However, this arrangement was not acceptable to the European powers, and the treaties that ended World War I provided for something different.

The agreement reached at the San Remo Conference stated that Syria had to recognize the independence of Lebanon, accept the French mandate, and remain dependent on France for military and economic assistance. France would be in charge of Syria's foreign policy. Other than that, however, Faisal was allowed to rule his nation with minimal interference from France. France considered these quite generous terms, and the relationship between Faisal's government and France was reasonably cordial in the beginning. However, in 1920, the French prime minister, Georges Clémenceau, who had made these arrangements, was replaced by Alexandre Millerand. Millerand's government took a much more interventionist stance in Syria.

If Faisal had hoped for some support from the British, he was disappointed. After the mandates were finalized at San Remo, the British pulled out of Syria, leaving France to deal with their own mandates as they saw fit. Hardline Arab nationalists urged Faisal to declare complete independence from the French. Cooler heads suggested he seek some kind of compromise that would preserve the Syrian kingdom while still satisfying the French. Faisal made gestures of cooperation, but the Syrian Congress insisted on total independence.

The French made several demands, including Syria's unconditional acceptance of the mandate, a dramatic reduction of the Syrian army and military occupation by the French, and punishments for Syrians who were implicated in hostile acts toward the French. Faisal tried to negotiate, but the French were unwilling to compromise, and before

Faisal had time to accept their terms unconditionally, French troops moved into Damascus. In July 1920, they overthrew the nationalist government and sent Faisal into exile.

The strength of the resistance in Syria was likely due as much to a sense of resentment toward the French as to dedication to an Arab nationalism. However, the French were careful to divide the nation into regions that lessened the likelihood of the development or organization of any nationalist sentiment.

Trouble in Iraq

Meanwhile, Britain was having troubles in their mandate. From the beginning, the British had not had a very organized policy in Iraq. They thought of the mandate system as a way to influence a region and prepare it for eventual independence—a sort of colonialism-lite. But again, in managing and organizing the country, they gave little thought to the desires or loyalties of the inhabitants.

The non-Arab people who lived there didn't care for British rule any more than anyone else did, but they did prefer it to rule by Arabs. The Arabs were happy to be free of Ottoman rule but resented that the country was being ruled by non-Arabs. The British had encouraged Arab nationalism when it was in their interest to do so during the war, but now nationalism was becoming a problem.

In 1920, the Arabs—Shiites and Sunnis, opposing Muslim sects, working together for once in their mutual desire for independence from the British—staged a revolt against the British occupiers. This conflict left over two thousand British and eight thousand Iraqis dead or wounded.

Despite agreement over what kind of rule they didn't want, the revolutionaries never came to much agreement over what they did want. As a result, the revolt did not succeed in booting out the British. It did have two important results, however. First, it birthed a kind of *Iraqi* nationalism. Second, it convinced the British that a more indirect rule in Iraq would be prudent.

The British decided to establish an Iraqi government in Baghdad, but one still under the authority of the British. The British seemed to see it as a government on training wheels. The new government was a monarchy, and they offered the kingship of it to Faisal. It is possible that this was done out of some lingering sense of responsibility for the promises they had made in exchange for his support during the war. However, it is also likely that they realized that his nationalist sentiments would appeal to the people. They also knew him to be a moderate man willing to cooperate with the British, as he had done with the French—at least during the time of Clemenceau, and probably would have continued to do with Millerand had the Syrian Congress not forced his hand. By this time, the British were suffering economically at home as a result of the war and really did not want to sink too much time and money into the administration of Iraq. Their role became primarily advisory. They did, however, want to preserve their economic interests there; the country had a great deal of untapped oil. The British needed a military presence to protect their economic interests as well as their routes from the Suez.

The Iraqi people were still quite resentful of the British presence in their country, and after a while the British government dropped the notion of a mandate altogether and worked out a different arrangement. The Anglo-Iraqi Treaty, signed in 1930, gave the Iraqi government complete control over internal affairs of the nation but gave Britain military rights in the case of war. The treaty also explicitly stated that Britain planned to eventually leave the country entirely. Though the British did step out of the internal affairs of Iraq, they continued to insist that Iraq's foreign policy align with British interests. King Faisal, however, was left with the task of uniting the many factions in his country in a single sense of nationhood, which he managed with some success.

Faisal was a moderate, humane ruler who envisioned a moderate and tolerant Iraq. He opposed sectarianism. The Shia (one branch of Islam) were a majority in the country (though a minority of all Muslims), and they resented being ruled by Sunni (another branch of Islam) elites. Faisal tried to reach out to the Shia, but with limited success. Under Faisal's rule, Iraq was the first Arab nation to get out from under mandatory rule, and they joined the **League of Nations** in 1932. In his biography of Faisal, author Ali Allawi writes, "It would be hard to find an equivalent figure who combined the qualities of leadership and statesmanship with the virtues of moderation, wisdom and decency." When Faisal died unexpectedly in 1933, a few months short of fifty years old, his inexperienced son Ghazi, only twenty-one, inherited the throne, and the country slipped back into a period of instability.

In 1936, a military coup overthrew the government and established a military dictatorship in Iraq. From this point on, the military was the most influential power in Iraq, with control over most of the political positions and decision-making of the country.

Another Revolt in Syria

Things in Syria weren't going terribly well for the French either. A few years after Faisal was deposed, nationalist sentiment boiled over among the Syrians, led and instigated by the Druze, an Islamic sect in southern Syria that was angered by administrative and social reforms imposed by the French. The Druze had previously revolted against Ottoman rule, but this was the first time it was done with an explicit nationalist message, and the first time it spread so far. This time it was a true "Syrian" uprising, not just a Druze revolt. Syrian nationalists joined the revolt and it spread quickly to Damascus, and even into Lebanon. The French bombed Damascus heavily, and eventually the rebellion was put down—but not for almost two years.

After the uprising, the French tightened their control and took measures such as appointing French governors rather than allowing the Syrians to elect their own governors. They also made sure to isolate the Druze from Arab nationalists in other parts of the country. However, much like the British in Iraq, this long and costly revolt convinced the French that direct control of the country was probably not feasible, and eventually they began to manage their mandate with a somewhat softer touch, though it was a gradual process.

A Pan-Islamic Conference

Arab nationalists were becoming increasingly concerned about the growing influence of Zionism. In 1931, 145 delegates from 22 Muslim nations met in Jerusalem at a pan-Islamic conference. The delegates expressed concerns about right-wing Zionism and possible danger to Muslim holy places in Jerusalem. It was at this convention that a true pan-Arab sentiment began to emerge. Arab delegates held a separate

Arab leaders gather for the 1931 Pan-Arab conference in Transjordan.

meeting to develop a pan-Arab covenant. The covenant, as described by Peter Seeberg, professor of Middle East Studies at the University of Southern Denmark, outlined three main points:

> *1. The Arab countries form an integral and indivisible whole. Hence, the Arab nation does not accept or recognize the divisions of whatever nature to which it has been subjected.*
>
> *2. All efforts in every Arab country are to be directed towards the achievement of total independence within one single unity; it being understood that every endeavour which aimed at confining political activities to local and regional issues is to be fought against.*
>
> *3. Since colonialism is, in all its forms and manifestations, incompatible with the dignity and paramount aims of the Arab nation, the Arab nation rejects it and will resist it with all the means at its disposal.*

Also at this convention, the first pan-Arab party was founded, the Arab Independence Party (AIP), which was dedicated primarily to Palestinian interests but also to independence and unity of Arab territories. In 1933, the League of Nationalist Action (LNA) was formed. This group was the forerunner of organizations, such as the Arab League, that were active after World War II.

Violence in Palestine

By the early 1920s, the World Zionist Organization (WZO) had a worldwide membership of over seven hundred thousand people. Even then, not all Zionists—and certainly not all Jews—supported the idea of making the Jewish homeland in Palestine into a state, though this did become the official policy of the Zionists over the coming years.

The League of Nations had put a premium on self-determination, the idea that the people should decide what government they wanted. Because Arabs were by far the majority in Palestine—about 88 percent of the population at that time—they felt that the Balfour Declaration and

Headquarters of the World Zionist Organization in Tel Aviv, Israel, in 2016

the Sykes-Picot Agreement were invalid, since neither was supported by the majority of the population. The mandate had mentioned the "Jewish Community" several times, but it referred to Arab communities only as "the other sections."

As Arab concerns about Zionism grew, so did the violence in Palestine. In April 1920, months after Faisal was named king of Syria and hope had started to grow for the revoking of the Balfour Declaration, violence broke out in Jerusalem. These tensions became known as the Palestine Riots of 1920. The British authorities tried to get things under control, but the riots lasted for four days. When Faisal was ousted from Syria by the French that summer, many of his followers, who had come originally to Syria from Palestine, returned and began to fight in earnest against Jews in Palestine. The situation in Palestine was dire, but both the British and Palestinian Jews hoped that the new high commissioner of the region, Sir Herbert Samuel, who took office that same year, would make a big difference.

Sir Herbert Samuel had been raised in an Orthodox Jewish home in Liverpool. By 1920, he had ceased actively participating in the Jewish faith but still had a great deal of interest in and sympathy with the Jewish community. His appointment as high commissioner made him the first Jewish person in two thousand years to govern in the land of Israel. He was immediately welcomed by the Jewish community. However, many Zionists were ultimately disappointed with him.

In truth, it may have been impossible for Samuel to please them, for he had two perhaps contradictory principles: Zionism and liberalism. In service of the first principle, he opened immigration between 1919 and 1923, and brought many well-trained, socialist Zionists to Palestine. This time was called the third **aliyah**, or the third wave of immigration to what would become Israel, and it was then that many improvements in Jewish agriculture—particularly collective farming—were made, greatly improving the quality of life for the settlers. In service of the second principle, liberalism, Samuel was committed to representative government. With Jews making up only about 11 percent of the population, this would have certainly curtailed immigration. And because democratic institutions were specifically a part of the League of Nations' approval of the mandate system, Zionists could not oppose it. In any case, Arabs refused to participate in Samuel's suggested legislative bodies because that would indicate their tacit agreement to the mandate system, and by extension the Balfour Declaration.

Revolt and Upset

In the first decade of the British mandate, the Jewish community made a great deal of progress. By the end of the 1920s, Jewish population had increased to 17 percent of the population. Jewish-operated factories produced textiles, clothing, metal goods, lumber, stone, cement, and chemicals. The settlers also built agricultural schools and experimental stations, and were working on a number of updated farming

HERBERT SAMUEL

Sir Herbert Samuel

Herbert Samuel, a non-practicing Jew, served for five years as the British high commissioner in Palestine. Throughout his life, he had been a long-time supporter of the Jewish cause. In 1915, he wrote a memo to the British prime minister, H.H. Asquith, proposing a protectorate in Palestine that would allow for more Jewish immigration. He believed that support of the Jews in Palestine would help Jews all over the world to thrive both intellectually and spiritually. Nothing came of his proposal at the time, but his ideas and arguments did seed the idea that would eventually result in the Balfour Declaration.

However, despite his dedication to the Jewish cause, he also took seriously his responsibility to unite the various factions in Palestine under British rule. He made many concessions to the Arabs, including appointing Amin al-Husseini, an extreme Arab nationalist, as Jerusalem's mufti, a Muslim legal expert who makes rulings on matters of religion. Also, in his attempts at compromise, he slowed the pace of Jewish immigration to Palestine.

Though Zionists were in the end quite disappointed with Samuel's tenure, by most other standards he was successful. For instance, he oversaw a great deal of improvement to the economy of the area and worked hard to achieve some sort of cooperation between the religious groups there.

techniques that greatly increased crop yields, improving the diets of the settlers as well as providing income.

The Jewish community, called the **Yishuv**, had also created a health-care system, Kupat Cholim, that vastly improved the health of the settlers. The Women's Zionist Organization of America established several hospitals, clinics, laboratories, pharmacies, and a training school for nurses. Efforts to drain marshes and swamps also made a huge difference in the health of the settlers. The results were dramatic. The Jewish mortality rate fell from 12.6 per thousand in 1924 to 9.6 per thousand in 1930. The reduction in infant mortality was even more dramatic, dropping from 105 per thousand to 69 per thousand in the same period.

By the end of the 1920s, the Yishuv had developed its own unofficial government with mostly independent agricultural and industrial systems, and strong public education and social welfare systems. The Jewish people were gradually becoming a nation in attitude and spirit, even if that nation was not yet official.

Arab leaders were disturbed by all this activity, particularly the increased immigration and the large amount of financial backing from Europe and the United States. By 1936, anti-Zionist sentiment was high. Several Arab leaders joined together, calling themselves the Arab High Command, to protest Zionist activities in Palestine. They called for a general strike of Arab workers and a boycott of Jewish products. This led to a series of attacks against the Jews as well as the British, including on the trans-Arabian pipeline,

The Mikveh Agricultural School was one of many institutions established by Jewish settlers in Palestine.

an oil pipeline that ran from Saudi Arabia to Lebanon. The violence lasted from April until November of that year but diminished somewhat after that.

In this midst of all this trouble, a British committee came to Palestine to examine the situation and propose a solution to the conflicts between the Arabs and the Jews. The committee was headed by Lord Robert Peel and came to be known as the Peel Commission. In July 1937, the commission announced its recommendations: to abolish the mandate and partition Palestine between the Arabs and the Jews—a partition that would have given Jews an extremely small bit of land in the north of what is now Israel. London immediately endorsed the plan, while the Jewish population debated it fiercely, with some for and some against. The Arabs rejected the plan out of hand, and it was eventually abandoned. However, the episode set off another round of anti-British, anti-Zionist activity.

This time the Jews responded to the violence with the Haganah, a paramilitary defense organization that had been first organized during the 1920–1921 revolt. The Haganah engaged in terrorist activities against Arab targets, and provided unofficial cooperation with the British police to quell the revolt. For the first few years of its existence, the Haganah had been a rather loosely organized network of defense groups based in larger towns and several of the settlements. After 1929, the organization grew to include most of the adults and youth in the settlements, as well as some members from each of the cities. It sponsored training programs for members as well as officers, and maintained arms depots, which were kept stocked by a steady flow of arms from Europe. Between 1936 and 1939, the Haganah became an official military organization.

The Arab revolt was not successful in its aims of stopping Jewish immigration and forcing the British to turn the administration of Palestine over to the Arabs. However, the revolt and its aftermath made it clear that the Arab population was not going to meekly accept the British mandate and Zionism—and that they were not interested in compromise, as their rejection of the Peel Commission's plan showed. The intense suppression of the revolt by the British had only angered Arabs further.

TIMELINE OF ARAB NATIONALISM

May 1916	Sykes-Picot Agreement is signed.
June 1916	Arabs Revolt in Syria begins.
November 1918	World War I ends.
March 1920	Faisal named king in Syria.
April 1920	San Remo Conference upholds Sykes-Picot Agreement and Balfour Declaration. Riots begin in Palestine.
August 1921	Faisal named king of Iraq.
December 1931	Pan-Islamic Conference.
September 1933	King Faisal dies.
September 1939	World War II breaks out in Europe.
October 1944	Alexandria Protocol is signed.
March 1945	Arab League is formed.

In 1937, Europe was on the verge of World War II, and Britain could not afford to jeopardize the oil pipeline that brought oil through Palestine from Mosul in the British mandate in Iraq. Britain responded to this dilemma by proving that it could break promises made to Zionists as easily as it could break those it made to Arabs. In 1939, British colonial secretary Malcolm MacDonald prepared a statement, known as the MacDonald White Paper of 1939, stating Britain's intention of establishing an independent Palestinian state in which both Jews and Arabs would participate in government. The policy allowed for a period of a few years in which Jews would be allowed to immigrate to Palestine. After that time, Jewish immigration would be allowed only with the agreement of the Arabs and land sales to Jews would be restricted. This was a particularly bad time to restrict Jewish immigration, as many Jews were desperate to escape Europe because of the tremendous increase in anti-Semitism and pogroms against Jews. The Haganah responded with demonstrations against the policy in support of illegalizing immigration.

3

Two Cultures and Their Struggles

The cultures and history of those nations being fought for by Arab nationalists and Zionists have deep and fascinating roots. The language, science, and art of Arab and Jewish culture, as well as the very lands where they live, contributed to their sense of unity and desire for a homeland. However, the attitudes and the needs of other people, both in the region and out of it, made it hard for them to achieve their aims.

Renaissance of the Hebrew Language

Zionism not only created a nation, it gave that nation a language. At the beginning of the Zionist movement, the Hebrew language had been essentially dead for two thousand years—used only for prayers and the study of religious texts,

Opposite: *A young woman reads the Torah at her bat mitzvah, the religious initiation ceremony for Jewish girls.*

and not spoken as a daily language since Biblical times. By 1921, Hebrew had been revived into a living language, and is now, along with Arabic, one of the official languages of Israel. This is no small achievement.

The first Jewish settlers of the twentieth century came to Palestine from many different countries, speaking many different languages—German, French, Polish, English, and Yiddish. If the community was going to be successful, it needed a common language. Hebrew was chosen in part because of its connection with the history of the Jewish people, but it was also a good choice for a practical reason: No matter what language Jews spoke in the countries they came from, most of them were at least familiar with Hebrew from reciting their prayers. Nonetheless, making Hebrew the common language spoken by everyone in the community was a difficult task.

In the early days of Zionism, several Hebrew journals were published in Russia, but reading a language is not the same as speaking it, and if Hebrew were to become the language of the Jews, Jews needed to know how to speak it. Eliezer Ben-Yehuda, a Russian Jew who published a Hebrew journal and settled with his family in Palestine in the nineteenth century, is considered the father of the modern-day Hebrew language. He began speaking to his family only in Hebrew. If they responded in Russian or in Yiddish, he would pretend that he couldn't hear them. They soon learned to speak the language. His was the first modern-Hebrew-speaking household.

Many Jews thought it was profane to use the holy language for the mundane activities of daily life, but Ben-Yehuda wasn't deterred. He published a dictionary of Hebrew, and included words that he invented for objects and concepts that did not exist the last time the language was used for any purpose other than reading and commenting on scriptures. Soon educators saw the value of Ben-Yehuda's project. The language was taught in schools, and many parents learned to speak it from their children. When the Hebrew University opened in 1925, all the classes were taught in Hebrew. The language that was all but dead in 1880 is now an official language of the nation of Israel. At the time of the Bible and the Talmud, Hebrew had about fifty thousand words; now it has more than two hundred thousand words.

Speakers of the Dād

Language was not only necessary in establishing the nation of Israel; it played a role in Arab nationalism as well. The Arabic language is incredibly important to followers of the Islamic faith. The Prophet Muhammad, the founder of Islam, spoke Arabic, and Muslims believe that God dictated the Quran, the holy scriptures of Islam, to Muhammad directly in Arabic. The Sunnah, part of Islamic law, is based on the Prophet's own words and is therefore also in Arabic. Many Muslims believe that understanding and reflecting upon the Quran in the original Arabic is an essential part of their faith. Often the efforts of colonial powers to replace the local

Writing is often a feature of painting and architectural decoration in Islamic art.

Arabic language with their own languages were thought to be a means of weakening the Islamic faith.

However, the importance of Arabic to the Arab nationalist movement goes well beyond religion. Many of the early Arab nationalists, a movement that was primarily secular, embraced the importance of the Arabic language. The young Arab nationalists whose movement was founded as a call for Arab rights in response to the Young Turk's movement for Turkish rights, the leaders of al-Fatat, first called their organization the Society of *Dād* Speakers. *Dād* is a consonant sound unique to the Arab language, and the term can be used as a shorthand for the language. The phrase "speakers of the *Dād*" is a way not only of referring to all the people who speak Arabic, but also of alluding to their shared identity as Arabs.

Of course, language is crucial to the development and preservation of any culture. With Arabs living in many different lands under many different rulers, any attempt to unite them into a nation would be dependent on their shared language. Maintaining a traditional language and not fully adopting the language of colonizers is an essential means of resisting colonization. Colonial powers will often pressure the people in lands they've colonized to adopt the colonial language, and even suppress the native language. So as the Arab nationalist movement grew during the mandate years, so did the emphasis on preserving the language and uniting speakers of the *Dād*.

The Golden Age of Arab Civilization

Nationalist movements are very often based in a yearning for a return to the greatness of a past civilization, and Arab nationalism is no exception. Where Arabs may be exceptional is in the accomplishments of that past. Arabs do indeed have a great civilization to remember.

Just like the view of many leaders of the Arab nationalist movement, during the years that the Arab empire flourished, being Arab meant being from the Arabic-speaking world, not necessarily from any particular nation in that world. This included not only Muslims but Christians and Jews as well. It was a true melting pot of cultures and was intellectually

SUNNI OR SHIA

Islam was established by the Prophet Muhammad in the early seventh century. After Muhammad died, his followers disagreed about how to choose the next leader of the faith. One group thought that only descendants of the Prophet should be allowed to become the spiritual leader. Others thought that the followers should choose their new leader from among the Prophet's most faithful followers.

The two groups became the two main sects of Islam that exist today: Sunni and Shia. The name Sunni comes from the Arabic phrase *Ahl al-Sunnah*, which means "people of the tradition." Sunnis stress the importance of following what the Prophet Muhammad said and taught. Shia Muslims (called Shiites) also give weight to what the Prophet's descendants say. For the most part, their religious beliefs are the same—both sects worship Allah, revere Mohammad, study the Quran, and fast and pray in roughly the same fashion. There are some differences, however, in how they interpret Islamic law.

At present, 1.6 billion people are Muslims, and very nearly all of them (around 85 to 90 percent) are Sunni. Shia Muslims make up the majority in Iran, Iraq, Bahrain, Azerbaijan, and Yemen. There are also large communities of Shiites in Afghanistan, India, Kuwait, Lebanon, Pakistan, Qatar, Syria, Turkey, Saudi Arabia, and the United Arab Emirates (UAE), though none of these countries is majority Shia. One of the reasons the two sects have trouble getting along is that in countries where Sunnis have governed, Shiites have tended to be poor and often the victims of discrimination and oppression.

open to learning from any place where learning could be found. Like most civilizations that encompass so many people, there were sometimes tensions between the different groups. However, this diversity was in part what gave the civilization its energy and enthusiasm, because there were so many different voices and traditions to draw on.

Between the seventh and the thirteenth centuries, which was the golden age of Arab civilization, learning and culture flourished in an Arab empire that stretched from Spain to China. Beautiful architecture, great literature, and innovative science were hallmarks of the Arab world during this period. The lute and the *rebab*, an ancestor of today's violin, can be traced back to Arab civilization. Three of the seven wonders of the Ancient World were in the Arab world: the Great Pyramid at Giza, the Lighthouse in Alexandria in Egypt, and the Hanging Gardens of Babylon in Iraq. Many **mosques**, palaces, and cathedrals were also built in the Arab world.

The world's first university was established in 859 CE in Fez, Morocco, by two Muslim women, and it was there that the practice began of awarding degrees for accomplishment in a given field of study. Women were allowed to study in many Muslim universities.

During the dark ages in Europe, much of the world's learning was preserved in libraries and universities in Morocco and Egypt. Many new scientific discoveries and advancements were also made. Perhaps the most important was the concept of zero, without which modern science and mathematics would not be possible. Algebra was also invented by an Arab, and many of the tools of navigation were developed in the Arab world. In 872 CE the Ahmad ibn Tulun hospital was built in Cairo, Egypt. It was a secular institution that served all people, rich and poor, Muslim and non-Muslim.

Arab medicine made great advances in the understanding of the causes of disease. A tenth-century Arab surgeon wrote a thirty-volume medical text that was translated into many European languages. Though those days were long gone by the twentieth century, the Golden Age was and is a source of great pride to Arabs.

Anti-Semitism and World War I

In the 1930s and 1940s, German Nazis took anti-Semitism to its greatest extreme, but they did not invent it. Discrimination against and often hatred of Jews goes back to Biblical times when the Hebrew people were sometimes persecuted for refusing to adopt the local religions of the kingdoms in the Middle East. Later in the Roman Empire, especially after the Roman emperors converted to Christianity, Jews were often persecuted.

Modern anti-Semitism and the term itself dates to 1873 when Wilhelm Marr, a German agitator, wrote *The Victory of Judaism over Germandom*, a hateful and paranoid treatise that claimed that "the Jewish spirit and consciousness have overtaken the world." He formed an organization called the League of Anti-Semites, the first political organization based on hatred of Jews. However, that movement might have died out or been overcome and the Holocaust never happened had it not been for World War I.

Though almost one hundred thousand patriotic Jewish soldiers fought in the German army in World War I, after Germany's humiliating defeat many Germans tried to place the blame for the nation's loss on Jews, accusing them, as a group, of treachery that led ultimately to Germany's defeat. In the economic devastation that followed the war, it was easy for people who were already anti-Semites to spread lies and incite hatred for Jews, and use Jews as scapegoats in Germany's own nationalist agenda. Germany's defeat in World War I radicalized young Adolf Hitler and contributed to the development of his obsessive hatred for Jews. Hitler came to believe—and convinced many others—that the only way to restore Germany to its former greatness was to eliminate Jews.

The Holy City

Three of the world's great religions, Islam, Judaism, and Christianity, trace their history back to the same city and the same man, Abraham. In Hebrew, Jerusalem is called Yerushalayim. In Arabic, it is al-Quds (which means "the Holy"). It is one of the oldest cities in the world, dating back to 3000 BCE.

The heart of Jerusalem is Old City, a maze of streets and alleys that connect the four sectors of the city: Muslim,

The Dome of the Rock mosque in Jerusalem is the oldest surviving Islamic monument.

Christian, Jewish, and Armenian (Armenians are also Christian, so this sector is also Christian). The historic buildings in each of Jerusalem's four sectors reflect these cultures, as do the foods, the languages, and the prayers recited there.

The Dome of the Rock, in the Muslim quarter, is a beautiful shrine built over a sacred stone. It is considered holy to all Christians, Muslims, and Jews. Muslims believe that the sacred stone is the place from which Muhammad ascended to heaven. The nearby al-Aqsa Mosque is the third-holiest site in Islam, after Mecca and Medina. Muslims often make pilgrimages to the site, especially during the Muslim holy month of Ramadan, when every Friday thousands of Muslims come to worship there. Jews believe that this is the place where Abraham prepared to sacrifice his son (Isaac in the Jewish tradition, Ishmael in Islam), after God had instructed him to do so (God stopped Abraham at the last minute before he harmed the child). Muslims believe that this event happened in Mecca. Abraham, called Ibrahim in Arabic, is the father of the Jews through his son Isaac, and of Muslims through his son Ishmael. And because Christians worship Jesus, whose ancestry is traced back to Abraham as well, all three of the world's great **monotheistic** religions derive from the same man and the same God. In the Christian quarter is the Church of the Holy Sepulchre, one of Christianity's holiest sites. It is built over the traditional sites of the crucifixion, burial, and resurrection of Christ.

The *Kotel*, or Western Wall, is in the Jewish quarter. The wall is a piece of the retaining wall where the second temple once stood, the only portion of the temple that survived its destruction by the Romans in 70 CE. This remnant of the most sacred building in Judaism is now the religion's holiest site. Jews from all over the world come here to pray, and have for centuries.

The city of Jerusalem is precious and sacred to Muslims, Jews, and Christians. For many Muslims, Jerusalem is also a symbol of the Arab resistance to Israeli occupation. Israel considers Jerusalem its capital, though most other nations do not recognize it as such and maintain their embassies in Tel Aviv.

Home in the Kibbutz

Kibbutz is the Hebrew word for "group" or "gathering," and refers to a commune, typically a farm, that is based on equality, cooperation, and joint ownership of property. The first kibbutz was established in Palestine in 1910 by young Zionists who emigrated from Eastern Europe with a dream not just of settling in a new land but also of creating a whole new way of life. By 1930, there were twenty-nine kibbutzim (the plural of kibbutz) with almost four thousand people living there. The kibbutz played a key role in Zionism in the pre-state years, helping to develop the land and the economy in preparation for the eventual establishment of a nation state.

In the kibbutzim, everything was owned collectively and everyone was paid the same no matter what work they did. The kibbutz was a direct democracy; all members had an equal say in setting policy, electing leaders, and making decisions about the budget. The day-to-day management of specific issues, such as housing, education, and production planning, was handled by committees. Though most kibbutzim were agricultural, most had some industry as well. Under this system, the kibbutzim of the interwar years planted crops, established farms and homes, and, it is said, "made the desert bloom."

Jewish settlers gather almonds at the Rishon LeZion kibbutz in Palestine, circa 1936.

The philosophy of the kibbutz is that work has value in and of itself and no type of work is more dignified than any other. Kibbutzniks (members of a kibbutz) were respected for how hard they worked, not what kind of work they did. People worked at different positions, often in a system of rotation, so that no one was permanently assigned to one job. Women were considered equal partners, and any job in the kibbutz was open to them. Elderly people worked if they were able. Children were housed and educated separately from their parents. Members ate in a communal dining room and shared recreational facilities. The kibbutz society

ISLAMIC ART FROM AL-NAHDA TO HIP-HOP

The term "Islamic art" refers to any art that is a product of the Islamic world, whether or not that art is specifically religious. These days, many galleries and art historians no longer use the term Islamic art, but prefer the phrase, "Art of the Arab lands." In Arab art, poems are often written on paintings, ceramics, and even buildings. Because many Muslims believe that making representations of the human form is a sin against Allah, most Arab art is free of depictions of people. Intricate geometric motifs are common, such as the repeating, often floral, patterns known as arabesque. Westerners are probably most familiar with Arabic art though carpets. Intricate tilework, used both on the inside and outside of buildings, are another common and beautiful example of Arab art.

In the early twentieth century in both Lebanon and Egypt, there was a renaissance of Arabic culture called al-Nahda. This was a movement emphasizing nationalism and secularism, along with rationalism and a belief in the value of science. In Lebanon, the emphasis was on reviving the Arabic language and introducing new genres of literature, such as the novel and drama. In Egypt, the movement attempted to make Islamic institutions more compatible with the modern world.

Arabic art is still vibrant in the twenty-first century. Today, young Arabs express themselves and their culture through a variety of modern art forms such as photography, hip-hop music, and creative dance.

is committed to allowing individuals to develop their full potential yet demands that each individual take responsibility for and contribute to the community.

In recent years, kibbutzim have undergone many reforms, but in many ways the modern kibbutz is very much like the ones established by the first Zionists. For a while in the latter part of the twentieth century, it seemed as if the kibbutz way of life was becoming obsolete, but recently, kibbutzim have made a comeback, as more young families are choosing to live a rural, communal life on the kibbutz.

Oil

Before the twentieth century, there wasn't much need for oil. Oil was used for lighting and for lubrication, but it took very little to meet these needs. Whale oil was the most common oil used for lighting. Coal was burned to power ships and trains. By the 1900s, however, oil was the primary source of energy for industry and especially for transportation.

Just before the onset of World War I, the world's navies began converting their ships so that they could run on oil rather than coal. More cars were being manufactured and more roads built. Airplanes were beginning to be used both commercially and militarily about this time. In 1912, a British Royal Commission was appointed to study the availability of oil supplies for use by the Royal Navy. The commission stated, "We must become the owners or at any rate the controllers at the sources of at least a proportion of the oil which we require." At this time most of the world's oil came from Mexico or the United States, with a small amount coming from Romania and Russia. But the outcome of World War I provided access to new and rich sources of oil.

The first major oil source in the Middle East was discovered in southern Iran in 1908, then soon after, several other large oil reserves were found in other places in the region, including in northern Iraq, around Mosul. When the British and the French divided the map in the Sykes-Picot Agreement, oil was one of the primary considerations in determining which country controlled each region. Mosul had been a part of the French sphere of influence in the Sykes-Picot Agreement, but in December 1918, the French gave control of Mosul to Britain in exchange for other considerations. There was a great deal of diplomatic wrangling among the European powers and the United States about who would have control and access to the oil fields in Iraq and how the profits would be managed. It was agreed that no oil prospecting or surveying would take place until the various interested parties worked out how the oil would be allocated, an issue discussed at length at the 1919 Peace Conference. In the years that followed, Britain and the government in Iraq struggled to come to terms about Iraq's oil, but in the end, much of it was controlled by a British-dominated company for the next half a century.

In the long run, oil proved to be both a blessing and a curse to the countries of the Middle East. The wealth that oil brought to many Middle Eastern nations improved the standard of living for many people and gave these nations more political power. However, the presence of oil—suddenly an essential commodity for industrial nations—was a strong motivator for more powerful nations to colonize and otherwise interfere with the affairs of the Middle East.

Words and Pictures

The period between World War I and World War II was a fruitful period for Yiddish literature. Before World War I, many Jewish authors wrote in both Yiddish and Hebrew, and many readers could read both languages. Mendele Moykher Sforim, Sholem Aleichem, and I. L. Peretz were three of the most influential Yiddish writers before World War I, and they influenced many younger writers. Warsaw, Poland, became a center of Yiddish literature after the war. David Pinski, known for his novel *Dos Hoyz fun Noyakh Edon* (*The House of Noah Edon*, 1931), Sholem Asch, author of popular historical novels such as *Kiddush Hashem* (*Martyrdom*, 1919), and Abraham Reisen, poet and short story writer, who is known for the poem "May Kemashmalon" ("What Does It Tell Us") created some of the most popular and powerful Yiddish literature of the period.

Many Jews had immigrated to the United States prior to World War I, and they produced an abundance of Yiddish literature there as well—often writing about the immigrant experience but also writing with some nostalgia about the Old World they had left. Polish-born Joseph Opatoshu wrote

Isaac Bashevis Singer was one of the first writers to have his work translated from Yiddish into English.

many works that described the daily life of Jews in Poland. His most famous work is the historical novel *Poylishe Velder (In Polish Woods)*, written in 1921.

Isaac Bashevis Singer was one of the first Jewish writers to gain a large audience among readers of English. He was born in Poland in 1909, and as a young man he worked for a Yiddish literary magazine. In 1927, he wrote an essay,

"Verter oder Bilder" ("Words or Pictures"), arguing that vivid images and naturalism are necessary for fiction. Over the next ten years, he wrote more than twenty stories that demonstrated his point. He published his first book, *Der Sotn in Goray* (*Satan in Goray*), in 1935. That same year, he immigrated to the United States, following his older brother, the writer Israel Joshua Singer.

Isaac Singer wrote several works in direct response to the Holocaust. In some of his stories, he introduced a demon narrator, suggesting that human speech was no longer adequate to describe human evil. His short story "The Last Demon" (included in *The Collected Stories*, one of his most popular and widely available books), the narrator is a demon and the only survivor in the town of Tishevitz—all of the human inhabitants have been killed in the Holocaust. The demon narrator reflects on the fact that he, a demon, has been made obsolete by the emergence of human evil that has far surpassed supernatural evil. The story begins with the demon saying, "I, a demon, bear witness that there are no more demons left. Why demons, when man himself is a demon? Why persuade to evil someone who is already convinced?"

After immigrating to the United States, Singer realized that his audience would be limited if he continued to write only in Yiddish, so he began to have his books translated into English. He was immediately successful.

By the time he died at age eighty-seven, Singer had been awarded many prestigious literary honors, including the Nobel Prize in 1978.

4

Nationalism During World War II

In September 1939, World War II broke out in Europe. This led to yet another realignment of priorities and loyalties of the world's powers. Once again, whether or not the European powers supported or kept their commitments to Arabs or whether they favored Jews changed depending on the pressures they faced in other parts of the world. Nevertheless, both nationalist movements—Zionism and Arab nationalism—came out of World War II in stronger positions than they entered it, even though many of the individuals these movements were meant to represent did not.

Arab Nationalism with a German Influence

The military that had come to power in Iraq after the 1936 coup was extremely nationalistic, and its leaders were

Opposite: *Al-Husseini and Adolf Hitler met in Berlin, Germany, to discuss the role of Arab nationalists in Germany's war effort.*

enamored of Germany and the beliefs and ideas of the Nazi Party. There were still some moderate voices in the government and in Iraq's nationalist movement, however, including the prime minister, Nuri al-Said, who was alarmed by these nationalists' inclinations toward totalitarian ideologies. Al-Said believed that the best way forward for Arab nationalism was by cooperating with Britain. However, at this time the military had far more power than he did. The German government was aware of its influence on Iraq's nationalists and fanned the flames of pro-German and anti-British sentiment there.

In October 1939, Amin al-Husseini, having been exiled by the British from Palestine, arrived in Baghdad, Iraq. Al-Husseini was the head of the Arab high committee and the unofficial leader of the Pan-Arab nationalist movement. He had been courting support from Hitler and the Nazi Party for several years, though until World War II actually began, the Germans were not terribly interested in further alienating Britain by supporting al-Husseini. Once in Iraq, al-Husseini joined with like-minded, pro-German officers in the military. They requested aid from Germany for an Arab revolt.

The German government seriously considered al-Husseini's requests—he even eventually appealed directly to Hitler—but in the end, Berlin was unwilling to support a movement for Arab independence.

Even without German support, al-Husseini and his supporters in the military launched a war of liberation against the British. The new government they established, in which al-Husseini served as liaison with the Fascist regimes in Germany and Italy, refused to honor the British right to move troops from India through Iraq. The British responded with a military invasion of Iraq. Al-Husseini and other leaders were forced to flee the country.

Despite this defeat by the British—or perhaps because of it—the nationalist movement only grew. A pogrom was launched against the Jews in Baghdad, and hundreds of Iraqi Jews were killed. Many more Jewish homes and businesses were destroyed.

Al-Husseini and the Fuhrer

On November 28, 1941, al-Husseini met with Adolf Hitler in Berlin, Germany. At this point in the war, the German army had taken Leningrad in Russia and reached the outskirts of Moscow. It looked likely that it would fall to the Germans. The United States had not yet entered the war. Things were looking good for Germany.

When Hitler and al-Husseini met, they both expected Germany to win the war and the meeting was to discuss what al-Husseini could do to help bring it to a close. Al-Husseini suggested an Arab revolt throughout the Middle East to fight the English, the Jews, and the French. In exchange, al-Husseini wanted Hitler to publicly declare that he intended to eliminate the national Jewish home in Palestine. Hitler, however, didn't like the idea of supporting an Arab revolt. He did not think it would be successful and did not want to divert any of his resources from the battles he was waging in Europe. He did, however, promise al-Husseini that soon he would support the liberation of the Arab world from the English and the French. Hitler had already decided what to do about "the Jewish problem." He planned to murder all the Jews.

Divisions in Iraq

One of the challenges for the Arab nationalist movement was that few people in the Arab world had strong identities as Arabs. Most identified with their regions, sects, or clans rather than with anything that might be seen as a larger Arab community. This problem was no less severe in Iraq—maybe even worse there. During the years between the wars, as the French tightened its control of Syria, Iraq had become the center of the Arab nationalist energy. It had no ethnic or religious identity, having been more or less created by the British, who had little regard for the people who lived in the lands the map designated. Rather than helping the nationalist cause by weakening other ties, this situation made the nationalist project more difficult because the people had no shared identity to bring them together as a nation, and still clung to their local loyalties. For instance, the Kurds in the north wanted political independence in Kurdistan. They spoke an entirely different language and their Sunni Muslim faith was the only thing they had in common with the rest of the Arabs in Iraq. The Shiite Muslims in the

Native Iraqis from many different tribes and cultures were trained to serve as paratroopers in the British Royal Air Force.

south of Iraq tended to be suspicious of Arab nationalism, viewing it as another way for the politically powerful Sunnis to marginalize them. (The Shiites were the majority of the population, but the Sunnis dominated politically.) So even in Iraq, where things were relatively stable for some years under Faisal and the British mandate, the organizers of the

Arab nationalist movement faced a complex social situation that made it difficult to find a basis for unity.

However, as more people began to move into cities and towns, tribal ties did begin to loosen. In addition, an expanding education system provided an opportunity for schools and universities to educate young people about the ideals of nationalism. Increased literacy made it easier to spread the message of pan-Arabism throughout Iraq and surrounding countries in the Fertile Crescent. Soon the idea of nationalism began to spread beyond the Fertile Crescent, first to Egypt and then to North Africa. France had colonized Algeria and Tunisia since the mid-nineteenth century (1830 and 1881, respectively), and Britain had occupied Egypt since 1882. There had been pockets of resistance in all these places, but it was based in local patriotism and had a strong Islamist component with little sense of an Arab identity. Now, though, more and more Egyptians and North Africans began to see themselves as Arabs before any local or religious affiliation.

The movement by this point was spearheaded more by intellectuals than politicians, making it much more "pan-Arab," and less of an Iraqi or Syrian or Palestinian nationalism. Nevertheless, it was still difficult for the secular nationalist movement to make serious progress. Though many people in the region were losing their tribal loyalties and identities, certainly not all were. Moreover, tensions between people's identities as Syrians, Iraqis, or Egyptians often interfered with a movement for an inclusive Arab

THE BOMB

At the end of World War II, the United States used nuclear weapons against two cities in Japan: Hiroshima and Nagasaki. The technology had only recently been developed, and the United States was at that time the only country that had this capability. After Japan's surrender and the end of World War II, many people appealed for an international ban on nuclear weapons. By 1949, the Soviet Union also had nuclear weapons and neither it nor the United States trusted the other to end its nuclear program. Instead, an arms race lasting forty-five years had begun. During this period, tensions between the two superpowers increased and their weapons became more powerful and more sophisticated.

By 2017, nine other nations had joined the nuclear club. Though Israel has not officially confirmed or denied the existence of a nuclear program, it has been an open secret for decades that Israel has nuclear weapons. Most sources say that Israel has approximately eighty nuclear warheads. An email from former US secretary of state Colin Powell that was leaked during the 2016 US presidential campaign put that number at two hundred warheads.

So far, Israel is the only Middle Eastern nation with nuclear weapons. Presently, the United States is working with Iran to curtail its program to develop nuclear weapons. Israel has never used its nuclear capability to bully its adversaries or threaten its neighbors, and there is no reason to suspect that it has plans for them other than as a last-resort defense.

identity. But perhaps the most difficult obstacle to a secular pan-Arab nation was religion. Far more people identified as Muslim than as Arabs. Soon, however, those working toward Arab unity took a slightly different approach that proved much more successful.

The Arab League

In the early years of World War II, Britain, concerned about the growing anti-British fervor in the region and wanting to protect its strategic and oil interests, officially declared support for pan-Arabism. In 1943, a pro-Arab member of Parliament asked Britain's foreign secretary, Anthony Eden, if Britain would be taking any steps to promote cooperation among Middle Eastern Arab states toward the goal of creating an Arab federation. Eden responded that Britain supported Arab unity, but that the initiative for any kind of unity must come from Arabs themselves. This simple statement spurred a new effort among Arabs for, if not a single Arab state, then some kind of organization of Arab states.

In late September and early October 1944, Arab leaders from Egypt, Iraq, Syria, Saudi Arabia, Lebanon, Transjordan, Yemen, and Palestine met in Alexandria, Egypt, to discuss how Arab unity might be accomplished. There they signed the Alexandria Protocol, a document that created the League of Arab States, also known as the Arab League (officially designated in March of the following year). It was a voluntary association of countries whose citizens were Arab speakers

Representatives from Iraq, Jordan, Lebanon, Syria, Saudi Arabia, and Egypt gather in Cairo, Egypt, in 1948 for a meeting of the Arab League.

or countries where Arabic was the official language. The countries agreed to support each other in pursuit of their common agenda and in matters such as economics, culture, social welfare, and health. That agenda included freeing the Arab states from colonial rulers and preventing the Jewish community in Palestine from becoming a Jewish state. The league is still in existence today.

Not by Argument

Many early Zionists believed that assimilation should be the first choice of a solution to what was already called "the Jewish problem," but because assimilation was impossible, a Jewish state was the only option for Jews to live free and safe from persecution. As early as 1896, in his pamphlet,

"Der Judenstaat" ("The Jewish State"), Theodor Herzl, founder of the Zionist movement, explained why assimilation was not the answer and a Jewish state was necessary. He wrote:

> *We have sincerely tried everywhere to merge with the national communities in which we live, seeking only to preserve the faith of our fathers. It is not permitted us. In vain we are loyal patriots, sometimes super loyal; in vain do we make the same sacrifices of life and property as our fellow citizens; in vain do we strive to enhance the fame of our native lands in the arts and sciences, or her wealth by trade and commerce. In our native lands where we have lived for centuries we are still decried as aliens, often by men whose ancestors had not yet come at a time when Jewish sighs had long been heard in the country.*

Herzl argued that what he called "the propelling force" for the establishment of a Jewish state was the "plight of the Jews."

Other Zionists thought that assimilation was itself the problem. As Jews became more and more assimilated into European society in the nineteenth century, some feared that they were losing their identities as Jews. Some cited passages from the Torah, such as Numbers 23:9 in which God, speaking of the Jewish people, says, "the people shall dwell alone, and not be reckoned among the nations."

Assimilation also faced problems in the nineteenth and early twentieth centuries because of the increasing nationalism of the countries of Western Europe. Assimilating into a Western culture often meant choosing sides between, for example, Germans and Czechs.

Though Zionism had some powerful and charismatic supporters, it did not enjoy widespread support among Jews in the late nineteenth and early twentieth centuries. In the first place, it seemed not only impractical but absolutely unrealistic. Also, many Jews considered themselves loyal citizens of the countries they lived in—they were not only Jews, but Austrians, Germans, Frenchmen, Englishmen, Americans— and did not want to be accused of disloyalty. In his book *The Controversy of Zion*, author Geoffrey Wheatcroft argues that "Jewry as a whole was converted to Zionism not by arguments but by events." And those events took place, in the main, in Germany. When what had seemed like one of the most advanced countries in Europe fell into the clutches of a tyrant who set out to systematically eradicate the Jewish people, there no longer seemed any option but to create a state of their own, somewhere far from Europe. But for millions of Jews, it was too late.

"Jews Unwelcome"

Ironically, Jews in Germany before World War II were among the most assimilated Jews in Europe. However, that changed with alarming speed in the early 1930s.

Like all Jews in German-occupied areas, members of the Jewish security service in the Warsaw ghetto were required to wear a Yellow Star on their clothing identifying them as Jews.

In the years leading up to World War II, Germany was suffering a tremendous amount of economic hardship. A worldwide depression had damaged most European economies, but Germany had the added burden of having to pay large **reparations** to the victors of World War I. The harsh conditions of the treaty that ended World War I weren't limited to economics, however. According to the terms of the treaty, Germany had to give up a great deal of territory and was not allowed to build its military beyond the small amount needed to maintain internal order. The Allies who had defeated Germany wanted to make sure Germany wouldn't be able to wage war again. The German people found these terms humiliating. The loss of esteem as well as the genuine suffering caused by the economic conditions made the country susceptible to dangerous populist messages, such as that being spread by the Nazi Party.

The Nazi Party promised not only to restore the economy but to return the nation to what it perceived and promoted as its former greatness, and they used Jews as the scapegoats for all the nation's problems and dissatisfactions. Their message caught on quickly. In 1924, the Nazis were a small and insignificant party. In that year's elections they won only 3 percent of the vote. In 1932, they won 33 percent, more than any other party. Hitler was made chancellor of Germany in 1933, and soon maneuvered to abolish democracy and have himself made supreme ruler—or Fuhrer—of the country.

As dictator, Hitler didn't wait long before introducing laws that severely limited the rights of Jewish citizens. Even before the outbreak of World War II, four hundred anti-Jewish decrees and regulations were enacted. In 1933, for example, the "Law for the Restoration of the Professional Civil Service" was passed. This proclaimed that Jews were "politically unreliable" and not allowed to work in state jobs. They were also banned from many professions, professional organizations, and other aspects of public life. Universities were required to restrict the numbers of Jewish students they admitted. Limits were placed on how much Jewish doctors could be reimbursed by the government health insurance for their services. Jewish lawyers were not allowed to work on legal matters in the capital city of Berlin. In the city of Munich, Jewish doctors could treat only Jewish patients. Jewish civilians who worked for the army were fired. In 1934, Jewish actors were prohibited from performing on stage or screen. Signs saying "Jews Unwelcome" could be seen in many public places.

In 1935, the Nazi Party passed a new set of even more horrendous anti-Jewish laws, called the Nuremberg Laws. This legislation denied Jews German citizenship and forbade them to marry non-Jewish Germans. Jews were completely stripped of any political power or influence. They could neither vote nor hold public office. In addition to being excluded from most ways of making a living, Jews were required to report any property or other assets they had in Germany or in other countries; eventually the government would seize these assets. Jewish businesses were taken over by the government and sold at bargain-bin prices to non-Jewish Germans. Eventually, Jews were required to carry identity cards demonstrating their Jewish ancestry, and any passports still held by Jews were stamped with a "J."

The Nuremberg Laws defined anyone as a Jew who had Jewish grandparents, whether or not the person was religiously Jewish or even identified as a Jew. No matter what a person's beliefs, practices, or loyalties, if he or she were

FATHER OF A NATION

David Ben-Gurion was born in Poland in 1886. His father was one of the leaders of the Lovers of Zion. When Ben-Gurion was just twenty years old, he moved to Palestine and helped establish the first agricultural workers commune, which evolved into the kibbutz. When World War I began, the Turkish officials exiled him from the Ottoman Empire because of his Zionist activism. He spent some of the time of his exile in New York, where he met other Zionists and supporters of the cause. He returned to Palestine after the Balfour Declaration, having enlisted in the British Army's Jewish Legion.

When the state of Israel was formed in 1948, Ben-Gurion became its first prime minister, as well as minister of defense. He created a national army out of the many active paramilitary groups, and this army easily defeated the Arab nations in the 1948–1949 war.

Ben-Gurion believed that the new Jewish state was the resumption of the history of Israel that had been disrupted two thousand years earlier when the Romans exiled Jews from Palestine. He worked hard to assimilate new immigrants in the country, create a nationwide educational system, and establish successful new settlements. He took a hard line on defense, responding to Arab violations of cease-fire agreements in kind. Because of this, he was not popular with other Western leaders, but he was a hero at home. In 1970, he retired from politics to write. He died in 1973. Ben-Gurion is often considered the father of the nation of Israel.

determined to have a certain amount of Jewish ancestry (what the Nazis called "Jewish blood"), that person was considered Jewish and subject to persecution.

In November 1938, a carefully planned (but arranged to appear spontaneous) series of violent incidents against Jews erupted around Germany. In just two days, over 250 **synagogues** were burned, seven thousand Jewish businesses, hospitals, schools, and homes were trashed and looted, while police and firefighters stood by and did nothing. Dozens of Jews were killed. The night has come to be known as Kristallnacht ("Crystal Night," or "Night of Broken Glass") because the streets were covered in broken glass from the shattered windows of Jewish homes and businesses. The next morning, thirty thousand Jewish men were arrested—simply for being Jewish—and sent to concentration camps where they were eventually murdered, the beginning of a Holocaust that before the end of World War II would kill six million Jewish people.

Herzl had been right. Assimilation had done Jews no good whatsoever.

No Escape

Though the Germans encouraged Jews to emigrate, because the government took their property, it was virtually impossible for them to do so. Some Jews, those who had money and permits that allowed them to leave the country, managed to immigrate as refugees to other countries, but for most it was

From early May to early July 1944, more than four hundred thousand Hungarian Jews were rounded up and sent to the concentration camp in Auschwitz, Poland.

difficult if not impossible. In July 1935, thirty-two countries, including Britain and France, met in Evian, France, to discuss the refugee crisis. Few countries were willing to accept any more Jewish refugees, arguing that their economies could not support the extra workers and that an influx of Jews would only exacerbate anti-Semitism in their own countries. Only the Dominican Republic and Bolivia agreed to provide sanctuary for significant numbers of Jewish refugees.

Britain required that any Jews immigrating to the United Kingdom either prove they had jobs waiting for them in the country they were moving to or had sufficient funds to support them without a job. Britain did eventually allow ten thousand children of parents who had been victims of the Nazis to come to the UK. The United States required Jewish immigrants to have multiple "sponsors," and Jews were put on a waiting list for entry to the States. Some 340,000 Jews managed to leave Germany during the years before the war, but sadly, many of them found refuge in other European countries that were eventually taken over by the Germans, and they were killed anyway.

In May 1939, the *St. Louis*, a German transatlantic ocean liner, left Hamburg, Germany, headed to Cuba. Almost a thousand Jews had bought passage on the ship. Many of these people were on the waiting list for entry to the United States and planned to wait in Cuba until the United States admitted them. However, the passengers did not know (though the company that operated the ocean liner did know) that even before the ship departed Germany, the government of Cuba had invalidated all their visas and landing certificates. They were not allowed to land. The ship remained in the port of Havana for several days, trying unsuccessfully to negotiate with the Cuban government. While waiting in the harbor, in sight of Miami, some passengers cabled US president Franklin Roosevelt, asking for refuge. He did not respond.

In the end, the ship went back to Europe. During the return trip, in response to a public outcry prompted by press coverage of the incident, France, Belgium, England, and the Netherlands agreed to accept some of the passengers. However, over a quarter of the *St. Louis*'s passengers died at the hands of the Nazis in one country or another.

Of course, the obvious source of refuge for the millions of Jews trying to escape the Holocaust was Palestine. During the 1930s, around sixty thousand German Jews immigrated to the Jewish territory there as a part of an agreement between Germany and Jewish authorities in Palestine. However, as the decade wore on, the British made it difficult for Jews to immigrate to the Jewish home in Palestine. The British argued that the small amount of land allotted to the Jewish home limited the number of refugees who could move there. Restrictions on Jews buying property also made it difficult for the Jewish settlement to increase its numbers. Nonetheless, because of the increased persecution of Jews in Germany, in 1935 a record number of Jews immigrated to Palestine. The British administration there approved less than a third of this number of immigrants for 1936. The 1939 British White Paper severely restricted Jewish immigration to Palestine. Some Jews managed to enter the Jewish part of Palestine illegally during World War II.

Zionists had established a Jewish home in Palestine, but sadly, when they needed it most, very few Jews were able to make it safely there. However, the events of World War II finally made the rest of the world realize the importance of a Jewish state—not just a homeland managed by someone else—for the Jews.

UNITED NATIONS
NATIONS UNIES

5

The Birth of a Nation, and the Death of a Movement

Both nationalisms, Zionism and Arab nationalism, were major factors in the diplomatic and military strategies of two world wars and the difficult and uncertain period between those wars. Unfortunately, the concerns of these two movements have not been settled, even today. Arab nationalism, an intellectual, secular movement based on a cultural and linguistic heritage, has gradually given way to a religious movement based on fundamentalist interpretation of Islam. Zionism was successful in establishing a nation for the Jews but still struggles to protect that nation from its enemies and to justify its policies to the rest of the world.

Opposite: *Flags of the 193 member states adorn the entrance to the United Nations Office in Geneva, Switzerland.*

The United Nations Steps In

Though Jewish people had difficulty finding places to immigrate to during World War II, after the war, as the rest of the world became aware of the massive, systematic extermination of Jews by the Nazis, many other nations, including the United States, came to support Zionism wholeheartedly. However, Britain continued to oppose Jewish immigration into Palestine even after the war. In 1946, Irgun, a militant right-wing Zionist group, bombed the Royal David Hotel in Jerusalem, where the British Administration was headquartered. Almost one hundred people were killed in the blast.

The official Jewish leadership began a program of illegal immigration, secretly bringing in Jewish refugees by boat. Tens of thousands of immigrants arrived in this way, although many were captured and imprisoned by the British.

The situation in Palestine was quickly getting out of hand. In any case, Britain, weary of war and short of money, had lost interest in maintaining its mandate. In 1946, it granted independence to Transjordan (now Jordan) and announced that it would finally surrender its mandate in Palestine. This proved a bit trickier than it sounded, however. Once the announcement was made, Zionists, as well as US president Harry Truman, began to put pressure on the British to admit as many Jewish refugees as possible before the end of the mandate. Meanwhile, Arabs both in Palestine and in the surrounding region pressured Britain to stop any further immigration at all. Both sides of the conflict attacked the British garrison in Palestine.

The League of Nations, started after the carnage of World War I, had noble aims, but its specifics were vague, and it had relatively little enforcement power. When one of its members, Austria, was taken over by Germany, the league was unable to do anything. The league had been established to maintain peace, and World War II proved how ineffective it was. However, the principle was a good one, and the world powers did not give up the attempt. In 1945, the league was replaced by the United Nations (UN), an organization designed to do a better job than its predecessor of negotiating disputes between nations and working to maintain peace. Initially 51 member states agreed to a charter that committed the organization to working together to address economic as well as cultural and social problems around the world. Today the UN has 193 members, including Israel, Jordan, Lebanon, Iraq, and Syria.

The opening sections of chapter one of the UN charter says that the purposes and principles of the group are:

> “
>
> *To maintain international peace and security, and to that end: to take effective collective measures for the prevention and removal of threats to the peace, and for the suppression of acts of aggression or other breaches of the peace, and to bring about by peaceful means, and in conformity with the principles of justice and international law, adjustment or settlement of international disputes or situations which might lead to a breach of the peace;*

To develop friendly relations among nations based on respect for the principle of equal rights and self-determination of peoples, and to take other appropriate measures to strengthen universal peace;

To achieve international co-operation in solving international problems of an economic, social, cultural, or humanitarian character, and in promoting and encouraging respect for human rights and for fundamental freedoms for all without distinction as to race, sex, language, or religion; and

To be a centre for harmonizing the actions of nations in the attainment of these common ends.

"

The UN was stronger than the old League of Nations for several reasons—not least of which, the United States joined this time. Equally important, the UN established a security council, which gave a more powerful voice to the stronger, more stable nations. The new body was both willing and expected to take a leading role in the preservation of global security. Clement Attlee, who had become prime minister of England in 1945, took the problem of Palestine to the United Nations, giving the new UN its first big challenge.

Best Possible Evidence

An eleven-nation investigative committee, called the United Nations Special Committee on Palestine (UNSCOP), was assigned to address this problem. UNSCOP spent five weeks in Palestine holding hearings. Arab leaders boycotted the committee, but Jewish leaders fully cooperated because they were eager to gain the sympathy of the rest of the world (and rest of the UN members).

Irgun, however, had been active in the period leading up to this. In May, before the committee arrived in June, the group had stormed a British prison and released 251 inmates. After several prisoners were recaptured and hanged by the British, Irgun captured and hanged two British officers in retaliation. "We repaid our enemy in kind," said Menachem Begin, Irgun's leader and future prime minister of Israel. The British were aghast, but UNSCOP members were about to see something even more disturbing. A ship named the *Exodus-1947* left Marseilles, France, in early July loaded with 4,500 Jewish refugees who had been displaced by the war. Six British destroyers and one cruiser intercepted the ship and escorted it across the Mediterranean. A few miles outside of Palestinian waters, the British closed in and began to board the *Exodus*. The passengers fought off the British Army for a few hours. The British, using machine guns and gas bombs, killed three Jews and wounded many more. The crew of the *Exodus* eventually surrendered, but only after a British ship rammed the vessel and threatened to sink it. The seriously damaged ship was towed into the Port of Haifa. The British foreign secretary decided to make an example of these illegal immigrants by shipping them back to France under horrible conditions on what was essentially

The tragic story of refugee ship the Exodus helped convince the world that Jews needed a state.

a prison ship. Ruth Gruber, a reporter, described the scene in *The Ship that Launched a Nation:*

> "
>
> *Squeezed between a green toilet shed and some steel plates were hundreds and hundreds of people who looked as though they had been thrown together into a dog pound … Trapped and lost, they were shouting at us in all languages, shattering each other's*

words. Some pressed their faces against the slanted fencing and their bodies looked broken and distorted. . . . Women were nursing their babies. Old women and men sat weeping unashamed, realizing what lay ahead.

"

The passengers refused the leave the boat in France, and the French government wouldn't force them to. The British then sent the ship to Hamburg, Germany, and eventually the refugees were forced off it by British troops using hoses and clubs. They were sent to refugee camps in the British occupation zone in Germany. The incident was widely covered by the international press and created a tremendous amount of sympathy for the Jews, and a great deal of outrage toward the British. The members of UNSCOP were almost certainly influenced by the incident. It allowed them to see how pressing was the need for a home for Jews. The member from Yugoslavia said, "It is the best possible evidence we can have."

Partition

UNSCOP presented its recommendations, and in November 1947, the United Nations agreed to a plan. Palestine would be partitioned into two sections. Even though Jews made up less than half the population, they would receive a little more than half of the land, though much of that land was desert.

Two separate states—one Jewish and one Arab—were to be established. Jerusalem would come under international governance. British forces were to leave Palestine no later than August 1948, and the new states would come into existence shortly thereafter. The plan attempted to address the concerns of both groups, calling for religious and minority rights.

The new map looked like a quilt, with the Jewish portion spread unevenly throughout Palestine. This was because Jewish settlements were scattered around the area, but it made it difficult for the Jews to defend the borders of the land they were allotted. The Jews were also given territory in the north of the country so that they would have room for expansion as more immigrants arrived. Possibly more troublesome was the fact that a great many Arabs lived in Jewish towns, so the new Jewish state would have a large Arab population. The Jewish state was to be approximately 5,500 square miles (14,244 square kilometers) with an estimated 540,000 Jews and 400,000 Arabs. The Arab state was to be 4,500 square miles (11,654 sq km) with about 800,000 Arabs and 10,000 Jews. Jerusalem was a multinational city, but within the borders of the Arab state. That isolated about 100,000 Jews away from the rest of their nation and surrounded by the Arab state. Nonetheless, the Jewish Agency for Palestine accepted the agreement; the Arabs did not. Arab leaders argued that the plan violated the UN charter because it did not uphold the commitment to "respect for the principle of equal rights and self-determination of peoples."

Civil war broke out almost immediately. The Arabs had several advantages: they outnumbered the Israelis two to one; they occupied the higher ground militarily; and they were surrounded by friendly governments. But the Israelis were better equipped, better financed, better trained, and better motivated. The Israelis were fighting together for the nation they had struggled for for half a century—and they had nowhere else to go. The Arab nationalist movement had not been so successful, and the Palestinians were still a fragmented group from a variety of nations, traditions, and clans. The Jews won decisively, and many more Palestinians left their homes to become refugees in neighboring Arab states or in parts of Palestine still held by Arabs.

At first the Jewish population was dismayed by this—many of them saw the plight of the Arabs fleeing their country as not unlike the Jews fleeing Nazi-occupied Europe. The Jewish mayor of Haifa begged Arabs to stay. However, eventually, as more Arabs left, the Jews realized that Arabs leaving made room for more Holocaust survivors to come and settle.

Six months later, in May 1948, fifty years after the First Zionist Congress and thirty years after the Balfour Declaration, the state of Israel was formed. Now the Jews had a home—a state, a nation—but it was a nation surrounded by enemies who didn't believe the nation had a right to exist. British troops left Palestine and thousands more Arabs fled. The next day, armies from Egypt, Jordan, Lebanon, Syria, and Iraq invaded Israel.

War

Again, the Israelis were vastly outnumbered by the Arab armies, but they had almost every other advantage. The Arab states said they were working together, as Arabs supported their Arab brothers in Palestine and to defeat the Israelis. However, each Arab nation essentially waged a separate war to defend or further its own interests. In under six months, the Israelis had delivered a crushing defeat to the Arabs. When the dust had settled, Israel had more territory than it had been given by the UN, had more easily defended borders, and had reduced the Arab population significantly.

The neighboring Arab nations now had hundreds of thousands of refugees to care for. But Egypt had taken control of a part of Palestine known as the Gaza strip, and Jordan had control of the West Bank area of the country. Thousands of Palestinians who had fled their homes in what was now Israel settled in these two areas.

Israelis and Palestinians have been fighting wars over these disputed territories ever since. Currently, Gaza is ruled by Hamas, a militant Islamist group. Hamas and other militant groups based in Gaza fire rockets into the border areas of Israel. Israel has Gaza under a blockade, which cuts off the area from commercial trade, as well as many basic supplies such as fuel and food. Israel also controls the West Bank now, where almost three million Palestinians live. Many Israeli citizens have settled there, but Palestinians and many Western nations consider it illegal for Israelis to settle there.

Palestinian refugees fled to Gaza after the Israelis won the 1948 war.

Other countries—especially the United States—have tried to help work out some kind of arrangement that will suit both the Arabs and the Israelis, but it is a difficult task. Many world countries recognize Palestine as a state, but not many Western countries. The United States and most of the countries of the European Union do not, for instance. Israel doesn't think it will be safe if Palestine is given status as a nation because most of the Arab world does not think Israel has a right to exist and many Arabs have vowed to destroy the country and kill Jews.

Questions of how Jerusalem would be controlled, what would happen to the many Jewish settlers in the West Bank, and what would happen to the many Palestinian refugees also will have to be settled before there can be peace in Palestine. In many ways, the 1948 war—or as Israelis call it, the War for Independence—is not yet over.

The End of Arab Nationalism

After the 1948 war, it was clear that despite decades of attempts to create a viable Arab nationalism, the Arabs were not at all politically united. In addition, the separate Arab nations were both militarily and economically weak. The message of unity had not been sufficient to overcome local loyalties (and local resentments). Fighting imperialists was no longer enough to rouse the faithful, whose problems were no better, and in some cases much worse, after the European powers had given up their mandates and gone home. The

Egyptian president Gamal Abdel Nasser had more success than any other Arab leader in establishing an Arab nation.

nationalist movement turned its energies and its message toward a social revolution that aimed not only to unite Arab culture and resist colonialism but to bring prosperity and strength to the Arab world.

Arab nationalism found expression in the years following 1948 in two movements: Baathism and Nasserism. Nasserism was a movement inspired and led by Egypt's charismatic ruler, Gamal Abdul Nasser. Nasserism combined nationalism and socialist reform. Baathism was the policy of the Baath Party, a Syrian faction that also promoted social reform as well as the creation of a single independent Arab state. In 1958, Nasser and the Baath Party created the United Arab Republic (UAR), a union of Egypt and Syria, a first step toward a true Arab nation, and the closest the Arab nationalists ever came to meeting their goal. In the end, the UAR was unable to survive the internal divisions between its two founding camps, Baathism and Nasserism. It fell apart in the early 1960s, but Egypt retained the name until 1971. By this time there were relatively few Arab nationalists left, and they had little influence.

Some intellectuals, many of them working in the West, continue to write about and promote the views of the nationalist movement but have failed in their attempts to support potential nationalist leaders and regimes. The Baath Party still rules in Syria, headed by President Bashar al-Assad, but the regime now is focused primarily on running Syria and preventing its overthrow by the United States.

Sykes-Picot One Hundred Years Later

A little over one hundred years after the Sykes-Picot Agreement was signed, it remains a powerful symbol of how colonial powers considered only their own interests when deciding the fate of a region and the lives of millions of people who lived there. While claiming to prepare the way for self-rule in Middle Eastern nations, Britain, France, and Russia drew up an agreement that effectively made that rule impossible. Because most of these new Middle Eastern countries, created by what one journalist called "clandestine colonial carve-ups," had little social unity to hold them together, over the century since Sykes-Picot, it has taken

BAATH PARTY

The Baath Party was founded in the 1940s by a Syrian Arab nationalist, Michel Aflaq. Its goal was to overthrow European-backed governments and create a modern economy that would improve living conditions for people in the Middle East. In its early days, the party's slogan was "Unity, Freedom, **Socialism**." The primary goals of the party were secularism, socialism, and Arab unity.

Over the years, the party has experienced a great internal strife, changes of leadership and philosophy, and periods of being in and out of power. In 1953, the Baath Party merged with the Arab Socialist Party and became the Arab Socialist Baath Party. Military officers in the party, such as Hafez al-Assad, seized control of the country in 1963. Disagreements between the civilian wing of the party, led by Aflaq, and the military wing eventually caused a split in the Arab nationalist movement. Aflaq and his supporters relocated to Iraq, where they joined with Saddam Hussein to form the Baath Party of Iraq. The Baath Party in Iraq was led by Hussein until his ouster by the American invasion of Iraq in 2003. After that the party was outlawed there.

The Baath Party in Syria remains active, but has in recent years moved away from many of its guiding principles. Most of its power has been consolidated in the Assad family (Hafez's son, Bashar, is now president of Syria). Though there has been much resistance to al-Assad's government—some even within the party—most party members are still loyal, even in the midst of a long and grueling civil war.

dictatorial leaders, alternately backed and overthrown by Western powers, to hold many of these nations together.

As we saw in chapter 4, the charter of the League of Nations was committed to the self-determination of all nations. The League was the brainchild of US president Woodrow Wilson, and he described it as being "for the purpose of affording mutual guarantees of political independence and territorial integrity to great and small states alike." Unfortunately, the United States responded to the end of World War I by retreating into isolationism, and the US Senate, afraid that membership in the League would get the country entangled in European affairs in opposition to its own interests, rejected membership.

Most historians agree that the League was less effective without the United States. When Edward House, policy advisor to Wilson, heard of the Sykes-Picot Agreement, he said, "They are making it a breeding place for future war." Whether or not the Sykes-Picot Agreement was in the main responsible, House was right about war. As a 2014 article in the former news outlet *Al-Jazeera America* put it, "In the last 60 years, that vast territory—from the eastern Mediterranean to Basra on the Persian Gulf, from Mosul in what is now Iraq to the Arabian Peninsula—has hardly known a day of peace."

In some ways, Sykes-Picot carried (and carries) more metaphorical than actual weight. The borders set out in the original agreement were shifted somewhat in accordance with the later needs of the British. Iraq, Transjordan,

The nations that make up the Arab world today (in green here) have still not found unity or peace.

Palestine, and Israel were all officially created after World War I. Yet as a symbol of the duplicity of the West and of Western nations' refusal to let Arabs form their own state and determine their own affairs, Sykes-Picot has had an effect far more enduring than the exact specifications of the original agreement. This is evidenced in the rise of militant Islamic terrorist organizations, which use Sykes-Picot as a powerful propaganda tool to support attacks in the West and support the rise of a caliphate.

ISIL

The Islamic State of Iraq and the Levant (ISIL), also known as the Islamic State of Iraq and Syria (ISIS), began in 2004 as al Queda Iraq, then two years later renamed itself as ISIL. Like al Queda, the organization is an anti-Western terrorist group dedicated to establishing an Islamic state in the Middle East. Though the two groups have similar aims, al Queda, the founding group, disavowed ISIL in 2012 and condemned the group for attacking other rebels and harming civilian supporters of the opposition.

Though ISIL is not actually a state (and many Muslims argue that it is not very Islamist either), it is a highly organized operation that seeks to maintain control of the territory it seizes. It has a governmental structure and bureaucratic system not unlike those of the Western nations it seeks to destroy. It seized a great deal of territory on both sides of the Iraq-Syrian border, and declared a caliphate. Much of the group's income comes from the oil fields there.

Efforts by Western nations to cut off the organization's ability to sell oil and participate in world banking, as well as military offensives to limit its territory, have been somewhat successful. By 2016, ISIL had lost as much as 12 percent of its territory. However, its powerful propaganda campaign has been able to recruit many disaffected young people in many countries—including Western countries—to join the group, or just to wage terrorist attacks throughout the world on its behalf.

GLOSSARY

aliyah Immigration to Israel, from the Hebrew word "ascent."

anti-Semitism Hostility toward and/or discrimination against Jews.

assimilate To integrate with the local culture of the nation in which someone lives.

Bolshevik A faction of the Russian Socialist Party that seized power in Russia in 1917; a precursor to the Communist Party.

caliphate An area ruled by a Muslim leader (a caliph).

Central Powers The alliance of Germany, the Austro-Hungarian Empire, the Ottoman Empire (also known as the Turkish Empire), and Bulgaria during World War I.

diaspora The dispersion and scattering of a people, especially the Jews, from their homeland.

Druze A member of a small Islamic sect living in Syria and Lebanon.

garrison A military installation where troops are stationed, usually for defense.

ideology A system of deeply held ideas and beliefs that inform political or economic policy.

imperialism The expansion of a nation's territory or influence by diplomacy or military force.

jihad In Islam, a spiritual struggle, often interpreted by fundamentalists as a literal war against unbelievers.

League of Nations An organization of member nations formed after World War I to help resolve disputes between nations and hopefully prevent future wars.

Levant The eastern part of the Mediterranean, including the region from southern Turkey through Syria to Egypt.

Maronite A member of a Christian sect in Syria and Lebanon.

monotheistic Believing in or worshipping only one god.

mosque A building where Muslims meet for worship and prayers.

pan-Arab Involving all Arab states, not always the same but often overlapping with Arab nationalism.

pogrom The official or organized slaughter of an ethnic group.

reparations Financial or other compensation made to the victors in war by the defeated nation or nations.

secular Having a lack of interest in or affiliation with religion or religious beliefs and practices.

socialism A political or economic system in which business and production is owned and/or regulated by the community as a whole, rather than private individuals.

sultan The leader of a Muslim country.

synagogue A building where Jews meet for worship or religious education.

Yiddish A language originally spoken by Jews in Eastern Europe, derived from a German dialect with elements of Hebrew and words from several modern languages.

Yishuv The name for the Jewish community in Palestine between the nineteenth century and 1948, when the state of Israel was established.

Zionism A nationalist movement for a Jewish state in Palestine, what is now Israel.

CHRONOLOGY

Brief Chronology of Zionism Up to 1948

1897 Theodor Herzl founds the World Zionist Organization.

1917 Balfour Declaration is issued.

1920 Chaim Weizmann becomes president of the World Zionist Organization; Herbert Samuel arrives in Jerusalem as British high commissioner. San Remo Conference upholds Sykes-Picot Agreement and Balfour Declaration.; riots begin in Palestine.

1932 Nazi Party comes to power in Germany.

1933 Hitler becomes chancellor of Germany.

1935 Nuremberg Laws are passed.

1937 Peel Commission issues its report.

1939 World War II breaks out in Europe. MacDonald White Paper is issued.

1947 Palestine is partitioned.

1948 The state of Israel is formed.

Brief Chronology of Arab Nationalism Up to 1945

1916 Sykes-Picot Agreement is signed. Arabs Revolt in Syria begins.

1918 World War I ends.

1920 Faisal named king in Syria. San Remo Conference upholds Sykes-Picot Agreement and Balfour Declaration. Riots begin in Palestine.

1921 Faisal named king of Iraq.

1931 Pan-Islamic Conference.

1933 King Faisal dies.

1939 World War II breaks out in Europe.

1944 Alexandria Protocol is signed.

1945 Arab League is formed.

FURTHER INFORMATION

Books

Gruber, Ruth. *Exodus 1947: The Ship that Launched a Nation.* New York: Union Square Press, 2007.

MacLean, Alistair. *Lawrence of Arabia.* Boston, MA: Sterling Point Books, 2006.

Zenatti, Valerie. *A Bottle in the Gaza Sea.* New York: Bloomsbury, 2008.

Websites

The Avalon Project (Middle East)

http://avalon.law.yale.edu/subject_menus/mideast.asp

This is a project of the Lillian Goldman Law Library of Yale University. The website contains original documents related to the history and diplomacy of the period.

The United States Memorial Holocaust Museum

https://www.ushmm.org

Visit here to see a living memorial to the Holocaust, with history, archival material, and learning resources.

Videos

Lawrence in Arabia and Prince Faisal

https://www.youtube.com/watch?v=WBsKGvm8pGA

View ten minutes of archival film (including stills) of T. E. Lawrence and Prince Faisal in the Arab revolt.

Promises and Betrayals

https://www.youtube.com/watch?v=JW2sm0iR0E8

This video details how British policy in the years between the wars contributed to the current conflict in the Middle East.

World War I Arab Revolt: Unification Usurped

https://www.youtube.com/watch?v=777zvUQPqeU

This eighteen-minute video discusses Arab nationalism and the collapse of the Ottoman Empire.

SELECTED BIBLIOGRAPHY

Al Jazeera. "The Two 'Isms' of the Middle East: Can Islamist and Arabist Ideologies Converge on the Issue of Unity?" February 4, 2008. Accessed December 2016, http://www.aljazeera.com/focus/arabunity/2008/02/200852518534468346.html.

Allawi, Ali A. *King Faisal I of Iraq*. New Haven, CT: Yale University Press, 2014.

BBC News. "Al-Qaeda disavows ISIS militants in Syria." February 3, 2014. Accessed December 2016, http://www.bbc.com/news/world-middle-east-26016318.

Borger, Julian. "The Truth about Israel's Secret Nuclear Arsenal." *The Guardian*, January 15, 2014. Accessed December 2016, https://www.theguardian.com/world/2014/jan/15/truth-israels-secret-nuclear-arsenal.

Cleveland, William L. *The Making of an Arab Nationalist: Ottomanism and Arabism in the Life and Thought of Sati' al-Husri*. Princeton, MA: Princeton University Press, 2015.

Friedman, Thomas L. *From Beirut to Jerusalem.* New York: Random House, 1995.

Fromkin, David. *A Peace to End All Peace: The Fall of the Ottoman Empire and the Creation of the Modern Middle East.* New York: Henry Holt, 1989.

Gelvin, James L. "Obsession with Sykes-Picot Says More about What We Think of Arabs than History." *The Conversation.* Accessed December 2016, https://theconversation.com/obsession-with-sykes-picot-says-more-about-what-we-think-of-arabs-than-history-58775.

Gruber, Ruth. *Exodus 1947: The Ship that Launched a Nation.* New York: Union Square Press, 2007.

Kaiser, David. "What Hitler and the Grand Mufti Really Said." *Time* magazine, October 22, 2015. Accessed November 2016, http://time.com/4084301/hitler-grand-mufi-1941.

Kramer, Martin. *Arab Awakening and Islamic Revival: The Politics of Ideas in the Middle East.* New Brunswick, Canada: Transaction Publishers, 2009.

McHugo, John. *A Concise History of the Arabs.* New York: The New Press, 2013.

Muir, Jim. "Sykes-Picot: The Map that Spawned a Century of Resentment." *BBC News*, May 16, 2016. Accessed December 2016, http://www.bbc.com/news/world-middle-east-36300224.

Rayman, Noah. "Mandatory Palestine: What It Was and Why It Matters." *Time* magazine, September 29, 2014. Accessed November 2016, http://time.com/3445003/mandatory-palestine.

Sacher, Howard M. *A History of Israel from the Rise of Zionism to Our Time*. New York: Knopf, 1996.

United Nations. *The Charter of the United Nations*. Accessed November 2016, http://www.un.org/en/charter-united-nations.

Viorst, Milton. *Zionism: The Birth and Transformation of an Ideal*. New York: Thomas Dunne Books/St. Martin's Press, 2016.

Wheatcroft, Geoffrey. *The Controversy of Zion*. Boston: Addison-Wesley, 1996.

INDEX

Page numbers in **boldface** are illustrations. Entries in **boldface** are glossary terms.

ABOUT THE AUTHOR

Avery Elizabeth Hurt is the author of many books for children and young adults, mostly about social studies and science. She didn't understand the problems of the Middle East until she grew up and met people who lived there. Then she realized these were human problems as well as political ones.